WINNING BODY LANGUAGE

Control the Conversation, Command Attention, and Convey the Right Message— Without Saying a Word

Mark Bowden

New York   Chicago   San Francisco   Lisbon   London   Madrid   Mexico City
Milan   New Delhi   San Juan   Seoul   Singapore   Sydney   Toronto

The **McGraw·Hill** Companies

2 3 4 5 6 7 8 9 0   WFR/WFR   1 5 4 3 2 1 0

ISBN   978-0-07-170057-3
MHID 0-07-170057-9

McGraw-Hill books are available at special quantity discounts to use as premiums and sales promotions, or for use in corporate training programs. To contact a representative please e-mail us at bulksales@mcgraw-hill.com.

This book is printed on acid-free paper.

To Pig

Contents

Preface

I get referred from client to client because of the results I get. Thanks to my reputation as a master of both verbal and nonverbal communication, when I walk into the room and begin to talk, there is already a preestablished high level of trust. We can begin working immediately, and my clients typically reach their goals at speed. And so I will spare you from any attempt to prove the credibility of my techniques with anything more than my personal views on their validity, based on my depth of research, knowledge, and, most important, long experience in the varied fields of arts, science, and entertainment, all of which converge for me in the relatively new field of *embodied cognition* (how the human mind is determined by the human form). My mission is to demonstrate, and train audiences around the world in the everyday practical application of this new angle on communication and its powerfully persuasive and influential effects on business.

According to one FTSE 100 company director, four out of five business communications fail. What this means is that most leaders, managers, entrepreneurs, and salespeople are having very little profitable impact when they talk to the people who matter most to their business. If you agree that communication excellence is a critical key to success in any business, and you can accept that an enormous proportion of human communication is nonverbal (it's often not what you say but *how* you say it that gets results), wouldn't it be useful to know how to instantly stand out, win trust, and profit when talking with your colleagues, clients, and superiors by using highly persuasive and influential *body language*?

If you want such communications as presentations, public speaking, team meetings, interviews and reviews, one-on-ones, water-cooler chats, and even media appearances to build trust and be profitable for everyone, including and especially you, then you can start *right now* to learn a new and powerful system for separating yourself from the crowd and communicating confidently by following the winning physical techniques in this book.

If you want to understand exactly *how* and *why* these powerful new techniques work, then read each chapter in depth, do the exercises, and get involved in the "Theory to Practice" case studies. These sections are evocative of common business experiences. They are here to serve as a further resource for developing your craft and your individual artistry in presenting winning body language. But if you simply need to know right now exactly *what to do* physically to win trust, then you can skip the introduction and go straight to the practical "Chapter Quick-Study" and "Just Do This Now" sections.

The work that I am about to take you through is innovatory, and is extraordinarily powerful—even to the most experienced of communicators. It has also fast-tracked "lost causes" into confident communicators and turned the "pretty good" into the "pretty great." So, if at any moment you begin to feel like questioning a technique or its rationale, step backward, take a breath, *trust*, and just do it. You will then see for yourself how effective my methods are.

Now read on and send your body out to work for you!

Acknowledgments

First and foremost, there is John Wright, the master of physical story and my mentor.

Great influencers on this work are Shaun Prendergast, Glen Walford, Andrea Brooks, David Bridel, Jacques Lecoq, Phillipe Gaulier, Moshé Feldenkrais, Rudolph Laban, Ivor Benjamin, Huw Thomas, David Peacock, Derek Griffiths, Charles Darwin, Richard Dawkins, Howard Bloom, Sir David Attenborough, the Great Johnny Ball, the Royal Institution of Great Britain, Douglas Adams, Den, Ken Campbell, Robert Anton-Wilson and A.C. Mrs. Morgan, Mr. Mutton, BAPA Middlesex University, Dr. Richard Bandler, Cesar Millan, Bruce Van Ryn-Bocking and the Lizard.

I also want to thank my precious and loving family: Tracey (without whom this book would be utterly unreadable), Lex, and Stella; Dad's love of the natural world and Mum's love of picturing it; and Ann, Helen, and David.

For their support, I want to thank BNI Corporate Connections One; Rami Mayer, Malcolm Cowan, Brenda Zimmerman and Alan Middleton at Schulich Executive Education Centre, York University; Jennifer La Trobe, Alan Engelstad and Dr. Carl Moore at Desautels Faculty of Management, McGill University; Daniel Tomlinson, Simon Jermond, Martin Nelson, Thomson Associates, Cameron Thomson Group, Chris Ward, Marcus Wiseman, Andrew Ford, Peter Buchannan and TEC, Michael Bungay-Stanier and Box of Crayons, and Mike Coates at Hill & Knowlton.

For continually allowing me to experiment on acting students, I especially thank Central School of Speech & Drama, Mountview Academy of Theatre Arts, E15 Acting School, NSDF, Brian Astbury, and most prominently The Bridge Theatre Training Company, London.

For helping bring "theory to practice" in this book, I thank Chris Irwin from Schulich School of Business and Micro OB.

For their trust and hard work: all my clients, who can and cannot be named.

I also thank my agent and publishers: Ashton Westwood at Westwood Creative Artists, and my editors John Aherne and Joseph Berkowitz, at McGraw-Hill.

Introduction

It is so easy to forget the massive impact that your body language can have on just how positively or negatively you are perceived in business. Even so, for some people, the level of mistrust that they build and the amount of respect that they lose with their nonverbal communication makes no difference to them. So look, no one needs to waste precious time here.

Stop Reading Now ...

Stop reading now if you are part of a commercial company that has no competition, holds a monopoly over a vital product or service for a very large population, and is totally at ease with the level and style of communication that it has with its captive audience. Frankly, the techniques in this book are quite superfluous. You don't need to communicate more effectively—if at all. This book is simply not the book for you.

If you are in a position within your organization where you wield total executive power, with no threat of demotion, review, or overthrow (maybe you have taken control of the business using extreme force and in doing so have neutralized all opposition), it's a good guess that you have no real need to engage with your colleagues in a way that wins their trust and compels them to help your goals. The physical communication models for persuading and influencing others that this book has to offer you are totally pointless for you. This book is not the book you are looking for.

Finally, should you be planning on leaving the world of business to become a reclusive cave-dwelling hermit for the rest of your life, living off worms and moss, totally independent of any human interaction and society to help you further your personal goals, the unique nonverbal communication techniques contained in these chapters and never before delivered to the general public, designed to help you stand out and win trust and profit, will not enhance your new life. This book should be firmly placed at the top of your "must not read" list.

So, to sum up, for any purchaser of this book who finds himself totally unthreatened by the usual market forces, poor public perception, or difficult human interactions, and so is unable to see any benefit in exponentially increasing his ability to communicate using this unique system of winning body language to control the conversation, command attention, and convey the right message without saying a word—let's hope you kept your receipt.

For everyone else around the globe who is still reading, congratulations; you have come to the right place. You know why you are here: because you recognize the fact that the feelings people have about you and your work are fundamentally based upon what is communicated by what they see you do, and not from what you think and say—and that is the real issue.

Communication Is a Billion-Dollar Problem

It is easy to understand why poor communication can cost a company dearly; for one thing, it simply takes longer for that sort of communication to be processed and understood by others, and even then it is most likely misunderstood. With poor communication, unnecessary questions are asked, discussions become needlessly lengthy, presumptions are adopted, and goals are wildly compromised to accommodate the misunderstandings created by this whole arduous process. In the end, the benefit that was originally intended from the communication almost always gets squeezed out of existence, and a dry husk of a message is instead pushed onto an audience. Poor communication is the culprit that caused one top pharmaceutical firm to lose $253 million after presenting evidence at trial. Why? The jurors were simply confused, and they subsequently lost trust in the company's story. Since then, the same $22 billion organization has agreed to a second $4.8 billion settlement rather than risk alienating the court a further time. This is just one example of a company whose poor communication lost trust, business, and money for shareholders around the globe.

So What Is Your Contribution?

Are you keeping your communication tools sharp enough, performing at your very best. Whether in pure business dealings or in social shoulder rubbing, the lifeblood of healthy communication must flow through all parts and extremities of the system; otherwise, the system will get sick. And how will you get help? Without effective communication at our disposal, it is totally impossible to organize people. If the use of all forms of visual or audible communication were taken from you, then how would you even plan for getting together for the planning meeting? Sure, you would be left with touch, taste, and smell with which to synchronize your agendas, but as you can imagine, unless both parties already knew a tactile sign language, it would end up being a very messy conversation.

So individually, you and those around you may have great brains that come up with superbly intelligent ideas, but without communication, you are totally isolated. Your individual intellects can very quickly become quite valueless to any organization, because without your being able to integrate with the organizational system as a whole, the greater good for everyone cannot be served—and if you are not an asset, then you may be a liability.

Presenting like a Dodo

Charles Darwin wrote in his second book, *The Descent of Man* (1871), that "Ignorance more frequently begets confidence than does knowledge." And in a report from the year 2000 entitled *Unskilled and Unaware of It: How Difficulties in Recognizing One's Own Incompetence Lead to Inflated Self-Assessments*, two Ig Nobel Prize–winning psychologists from Cornell University asserted that people who feel that they are achieving in the top third in ability actually tend to score in the lowest quarter, grossly overestimating their performance.

For this reason, it is important that even seasoned communicators look to themselves whenever they become overconfident of their abilities. Everyone should take the time to develop and evolve their work, not only to fulfill their own potential, but also to keep their competitive advantage in a free-market economy, where "survival of the fittest" remains the model for evolutionary development.

Changes in commerce and society at large are inextricably linked to changes in the ways in which valuable information can be exchanged. So leading the pack and staying one step ahead of the rest of the big game in the communication jungle is not just linked to business survival — it *is* survival!

The Power of Communication

From watching other primates, one can expect that human beings first signaled to each other using simple gestures and sounds in order to group together, plan, hunt, and feed. As we physically and mentally advanced, our communication moved forward to include a fuller vocabulary of symbols and words. Small human groups or tribes could now look further afield, not only geographically in space but imaginatively in time, by laying down plans for the future, accounting for the past, negotiating the coalition of territories, or winning over the terrain through ever more elaborate strategies of aggression.

As the abundance of language increased, so too did the abundance of what humans were able to achieve with it, and as the ways in which language was able to be broadcast around the globe increased, so too did the power that language could have over vast swaths of land, and the people who lived in those lands.

It is the simple signs, sounds, signals, pictures, hieroglyphs, words, publications, and broadcasts disseminated across all channels and media, throughout time and space, that have revolutionized and advanced our world and our understandings within it. With our various sophisticated forms of communication, humankind has evolved into the major intelligent biological force on this planet.

It is worth noting that, on the flip side, poor communication has meant certain death for some groups that have been unable to sustain, or have lost control of, their communication methods, channels, or technologies, and so have disappeared or been subsumed by others—by losing the power of communication, they have often lost their political, social, artistic, economic, and ecological niches. For example, the decline of the Roman Empire could be argued as resulting from the collapse of their expansive, expensive, and consequently unsustainable communication network.

Human beings have evolved to such a degree that *we* no longer adapt to changes in our environment, but rather adapt our environment to the changes in *us*. What's more, we have developed the capacity to pass down to others the skill and knowledge on exactly how to do this.

The Art and Science of Communication

It is perhaps this ability to pass our skill and ability down through the generations that explains why the techniques, models, and processes that you are about to learn come from ancient traditions of art going back to before the first civilizations, starting with the first professional storytellers, presenters, or public speakers—the mediators between the physical world and the realm of the imagination—the shaman, witch doctor, or magician.

Now, if the idea of using techniques that are thousands of years old and were passed down orally from this lineage of tribal sorcerers seems a little freaky or out there or just plain hocus-pocus, then maybe you should pay a visit to your hedge fund manager and ask him, "What do you think for the market this quarter?" Now watch carefully as the dance begins. First the charts will be summoned up, full of lines and symbols that map the past knowledge of the ancestors and point to a place in time that does not as yet exist. Maybe disincarnate entities will be allied with to bring deeper knowledge to the fore. Sure, you can't hear them—they are, you are assured, on the other end of the phone, and they have insight into the declining equity markets way above and beyond the floor that you are currently on. They exist on a higher plane and bonus scale. Then finally, with the use of a tool that combines roots with floating points, a figure is arrived at and the bones are cast. "Go short!" is the answer. "Are you sure?" you reply. The manager nods sagely at his advice that you sell a risk that you don't yet own.

Can this modern-day soothsayer be sure? Well, the day of reckoning on this piece of advice exists as an event in the future, so it is therefore only a prediction of the future based on specialized knowledge of the past and the present. If artful storytelling has convinced you of the insight, then you might trust to fortune and buy in. No one knows anything for sure here. You are banking on the act and the actor—there is nothing "real" that you can hold in your hand and with which you can have security. As one anonymous Wall Street executive was quoted by CBS News as saying when the financial crisis hit in 2008, "Everybody is pretending to have some knowledge, some vision, because in fact money doesn't exist, it's a notional concept. Lose faith in the concept and you get chaos."

This is why the fundamental nonverbal art (image, movement, sound, and context) of the earth's first-ever professional story-tellers and every important performance innovation that has followed since are exactly what you will be studying in this book to help you win trust with body language in a very uncertain world.

Applause!

By evolving your communication ability through learning some winning techniques, you will become advanced in being able to share clear descriptions of your business, your vision and the barriers holding you back.

This book will teach you the power behind the world's greatest communicators, who know the importance of sending out clear and highly effective messages to all those around them, and who know the importance of *using body language strategically*. These powerful communicators know that the content of their message pales in comparison to *how they are seen and heard*. The unique system of nonverbal communication that I have devised, TruthPlane, is practiced by the very same top business and political leaders around the globe. By learning its gestural system and other practices, you will master a full vocabulary of gesture delivery including the universal secrets of persuasive and influential body language: a comprehensive and practical understanding of the signals that bind us all together, regardless of culture or sex, and that cause our messages to stand out, win trust, and gain profit with the people who really matter in our lives — the people who can bring us solutions.

The use of effective nonverbal communication can deliver unparalleled benefits to both you and your business, because effective communication reaps positive results: increased market valuation, greater employee commitment, involvement, retention, and morale; and stronger customer loyalty. All of this creates value.

Nothing happens without communication. It takes interaction between people to create an idea, a product, or a service, and it takes collaboration to implement and execute it well. No one works in a vacuum; everyone communicates in some way. But lack of communication means lack of opportunity and loss of profit. That's why improving your communication will improve the health of your organization, your company, your wealth, and your well-being. That's why you are holding this book: *you* get it!

Of course, bad business is also about useless selling processes that miss the mark by a mile, and about rambling, cryptic, incoherent e-mails that are misunderstood, ignored, or taken too seriously, resulting in hurt feelings, ill will, and crisis meetings, where the company's lawyers and a human resource manager deliver alienating advice on how to communicate better in future. But you are not here to get clever at vision and mission statements, news releases, financial results, product announcements or legal argument. This is not about internal newsletters, client appreciation notes or annual reports. These are all important and have their place, but they form just a fraction of the communication that takes place every day. This book cuts to where the heart of communication is—*body language*.

We will focus on nonverbal mastery for whenever you have to deliver your message live. Not only is making a live presentation the number one fear in business communication, but according to a *New York Times* study of social anxiety and the 2005 edition of *The Book of Lists*, it is *the* number one fear— period. In second place came meeting new people, and death limped home third. Even the greatest orator of the Roman Empire (and the man perceived as its most versatile mind), Cicero, said of public speaking, "I turn pale at the outset of a speech and quake in every limb and in all my soul."

Let's Begin

So now you perhaps have an even fuller awareness of the importance of communication to you in your business; you may also recognize that you've seen some people out there who are skilled at it. And some people who are successful seem to have something special about them: they captivate a room; everyone pays attention to them, and they benefit every time they show up. That's what *you* want to be able to do. This book is written to help you practically and substantially improve your ability to communicate and persuade. It ensures that you achieve real consistency and congruency between the messages you send verbally and those you send nonverbally. This book is about exactly how you can use your body language strategically to your advantage when you go about your business, and especially when you speak, present, network, or negotiate, to profit from all your communications, *starting today.*

Ago ergo cogito (I act, therefore I think).

—Motto of the University of Wisconsin's
Laboratory of Embodied Cognition

Communication Is More than Words

They Just Don't See What You're Saying

The single biggest problem in communication is the illusion that it has taken place.

—George Bernard Shaw

In this chapter you'll learn:

- The fundamental mechanism for all communication
- How we all know what we all know
- Why content is not king
- Congruence and the key to losing trust and business
- The most important person in the history of communication, ever!

B efore we get deep into body language, it is important to break down communication as a whole into its basic parts and understand the fundamentals behind it. This knowledge, the understanding of how communication actually works, is the starting line from which your real competitive advantage can really take off.

Human communication, reduced to its simplest form, consists of *a source transmitting a message to a receiver in order to achieve an intended result.*

So, to make sure that your communication is really taking place, first you need to make sure that there is a source (you), that you have a way of transmitting a message (using your body or your voice, writing, or some other method), and finally that you have a receiver (someone else). Oh, and there's something else that is too often forgotten: you need a reason to send the message, an intended outcome, or it will be impossible to form the communication at all, or at best it will be nonsense, because if you do not know the intended end goal of any action, you cannot hope to select the best actions to perform in order to achieve that goal.

Thus, the basic linear model for human communication looks like this: the source encodes a message and sends it via a channel, to be received and decoded by the receiver. Of course, there is also the inevitable feedback to the source. For example, as you make your way to a business meeting, you notice that a car is about to pull in front of your vehicle; as a courtesy, you hit your horn to alert the driver of that car of the danger to him; he hears it and, to your surprise, flips you the finger in return!

Clearly one thing to look out for is whether your message has had the *desired effect* that you intended, or anything close to the desired effect, on your audience. As the highly influential American communication theorist Harold Lasswell described: *Who (says) What (to) Whom (in) What Channel (with) What Effect.*

Talking Trash

If the specific communication has not had the intended effect, when you look for where your message has been let down, it is best to keep in mind the modern computational communication model described by the acronym GIGO (Garbage In—Garbage Out). This principle was perhaps first hit upon by the genius engineer Charles Babbage commenting in his autobiography, *Passages from the Life of a Philosopher* (1864), that when he was asked (by an eminent British member of Parliament, no less) whether the outcome of a calculation would be correct even when incorrect data were placed into that calculation, he could only reply, "I am not able to comprehend the kind of confusion of ideas that could provoke such a question!"

The observation is that if the feedback appears to be nonsense, it could well be because you fed in a stream of similar nonsense in the first place! In all communication, pay attention to the fact that it is a two-way system with a feedback loop. In other words, "the phone goes both ways," and any message can easily escalate out of control and spiral into craziness, and when it does, everyone is to blame.

Understanding the Message

On top of all this, according to Shannon and Weaver's very popular model of communication, while the message is in transit, it is subject to all manner of distortion, and understandings and misunderstandings are influenced by factors well beyond the control of either the sender or the receiver.

To illustrate, a simple but relatively comprehensive diagram of human communication looks something like Figure 1.1.

You can see the possibilities for corruption of the message and its meaning at every point in this model, either in the mind of the receiver through *generalization*, *deletion*, or *distortion*; or during the transit of the message

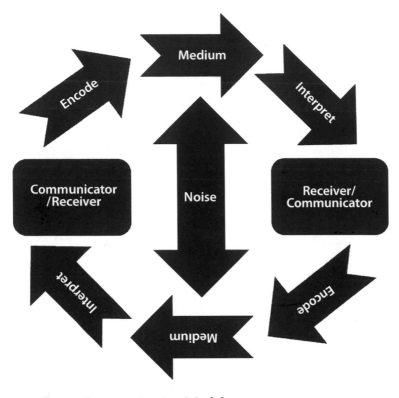

Figure 1.1 Communication Model

as a result of "noise" either interrupting, distorting, or creating an amplified resonance in the message.

So how do we ever get to understand a communication?

How We Know What We Know

Let's look at it from the viewpoint of an area of philosophy called epistemology, which deals in theories around the question, "How do we know what we know?"

At this point, you may be thinking, "Why should an area of *philosophical* study be so important to the business body language practitioner, who surely should be focused on the influential effects of physical action, the *doing* rather than the *thinking*?" Well, the answer is that if you know the exact mechanism by which people understand any communication, you will have a better ability to influence the mechanics of that conversation. By doing so, you will optimize your persuasive influence over the recipient's mind and the final outcome of the communication: bringing the receiver's understanding in line with your goals.

Simply stated, when you can comprehend the cogs and wheels of how we gain understanding, you can deliver understanding more effectively, just as a mechanic who understands the workings of an engine can supercharge it, or a programmer who understands code can hack it, or a bartender who understands the simple science of a martini can mix the best Manhattan in town.

So what, according to philosophers, are the major ingredients that make up the cocktail that we call "knowledge"?

Facts

Thought in this area is as diverse as you might expect from a discipline in which thinking is an end in itself. However, the debate tends to summarily lead toward two main ingredients: "belief" and "truth." Indeed, the great Harvard epistemologist and metaphysician Roderick Chishol defined knowledge as *justified true belief.* But what justifies the truth of a belief? Many would say that *facts* do the job—and as the eminent philosopher Edmund Burke once said of facts, "They are to the mind as food is to the body." So where does the mind get these nutritional facts, and why might some be more tasty to our feeling of *knowing* than others?

The word *fact* originally comes from the Latin *factum,* meaning "a thing done or performed." This definition provokes the question: how do we know, as certainly as we ever can, that anything has really been done or performed? The answer may be that we *ourselves* must sense it with one or more of our traditional five senses or potentially more than a dozen other exteroceptive and interoceptive senses. Certainly, this is the viewpoint of Aristotle and a line of thinkers who place *our senses* as the foundation of all fact and belief, and so of truth and knowledge. You might say, "We sense it, therefore it is." From this idea, we can understand that our senses, which form our impressions of reality, are our route to knowing that what is *out there* is indeed out there. Our senses are the exact tools that we use to form human understanding of what is happening in the world, and therefore what can be believed and held to be true and trustworthy.

Look Smart

However, in the business world, where the intellect is so often given the highest status, we would expect that we all know what we know because of how clever we are, not from what we sense outside of ourselves. In the top floors of an organization, those who occupy the "C-suite" are almost never referred to as the "sharpest eyes" or the "biggest ears," but as "the smartest guys in the room"—it is about brains and not body parts, isn't it?

If that is the case, though, then how do you account for Mehrabian's 7 percent–38 percent–55 percent rule? I'm sure you don't need reminding of it but for those who would like a quick review, here it is.

The Body Rules First, there are three commonly understood elements in any face-to-face human communication: *words, tone of voice,* and *body language.* The first category, the words, is known as *verbal* communication, and the last two categories, tone of voice and body language, are known as *nonverbal* communication (the focus of this book). The nonverbal elements have been found to be particularly important for communicating the information that forms a receiver's understanding of the *feelings, attitude,* or *intent* behind a communication. Indeed, this is true to such an extent that body language accounts for 55 percent of that understanding, tone of voice accounts for 38 percent, and the verbal content, the words, supplies only 7 percent of the perceived overall feeling, attitude, or intent that a communicator communicates. This implies, first, that the feeling, attitude, or intent that we might communicate is *almost entirely dependent* on the non-verbal message (93 percent), not on what we say.

What You Say

So, to put all of these psychological statistics on "silent messages" and the first insights derived from them into the context of business communication: when you are delivering any kind of business presentation, while your *intellectual content* may be delivered entirely verbally, the nonverbal cues are more than 10 times as important in your audience perceiving your *belief* or *conviction* concerning that material.

It's of very limited use for the chief financial officer to only *say,* "We've had a great year." To get close to convincing an audience of this, she needs it to *sound* (38 percent) and, most important, *look* (55 percent) to the audience like it is true. Indeed, it would seem from these statistics, first presented to the public by Albert Mehrabian (professor emeritus of psychology, UCLA), that in this case, when planning a speech, our CFO might be wisest to pay more attention to how she shows up looking like a good year has been had, than on the "It's Been a Great Year" speech she is going to make.

As American modernist poet William Carlos Williams wrote, "It is not what you say that matters but the manner in which you say it; there lies the secret of the ages." It appears that content is not king after all. But wait, there's more.

All Together Now . . .

More important, Mehrabian's findings also conclude that to produce effective and meaningful messages the words, sound, and body need to support one another. In the case of any incongruence, the receiver of the message trusts the predominant nonverbal cues (remember our voice 38 percent + vision 55 percent) rather than the potential literal meaning of the words (verbal 7 percent).

Given this second insight from Dr. Mehrabian's research, it is fair to say, in the context of the earlier hypothetical CFO speech, that if the words of the presentation say, "It's been a great year," but the CFO's body stance and the cadence (rise and fall in tone) of her voice indicate, "It has been a *lousy* year," the audience is once again at least 10 times as likely to trust the perceived meaning of the messages coming through the nonverbal communication; listeners will come away with the feeling that it has been a *lousy* year. They will not trust the words over the voice, or even the words and voice over the body.

From these findings, we can quickly deduce that in the case of live human interaction, we know what we know because *we see it*. In short:

We believe it when we see it!

Yet the C-suite, board, directors, executives, shareholders, stakeholders, clients, customers, interviewers, and the public at large are not prone to making decisions purely based on faith in what they say—are they? Well, get this.

Blowing Smoke

We now know from the scientific findings so far that if we see one set of clear physical signals from the body, we are far more likely to accept their meaning as fact than any verbal message to the contrary. However, if we already have a trustworthy base of knowledge in an area, and so the meaning of the words is considered factual, still without perfect congruence with the nonverbal message we experience a state of "cognitive dissonance," which is the mental anguish we experience when knowledge and belief collide and conflict. This is a point at which we often put our faith in *how we feel* above the intellectual data we have received.

As an example, let's say that we own shares in a particular investment, and figures show that the market is way down, our investment's share price is at rock bottom, and by all accounts the future is bleak. However, when we show up at the annual shareholders' meeting, we are served champagne in an atmosphere of jubilation. While we know that the picture is grim, and we have experienced information elsewhere to suggest that we should get out now, the feel-good factor we experience from drinking champagne in a party atmosphere, creates cognitive dissonance, potentially clouding our judgment given the feelings produced by the new physical experience. We may now feel that "it's going to get better," "there is some good news on the horizon," or "there is truly cause for celebration." And so we trust those shares further, perhaps unwisely and perhaps against our "better judgment," because of the feeling produced by the champagne reception. But of course, you don't fall for that type of manipulation . . . do you?

Here's another illustration of cognitive dissonance from the world of health and wellness that some of you may have noticed or even experienced yourselves: cigarette smokers tend to experience cognitive dissonance around the issue of how bad smoking is for their health. Medicine tells us how and why cigarettes cause lung cancer and can shorten any smokers' life expectancy, yet many smokers may not have experienced the physical effects or seen any physical evidence of disease or a shortened lifespan. Furthermore, as they inhale the cigarette smoke containing nicotine and additives, these complex organic chemicals enter the bloodstream and most often produce a physical experience of pleasure for them, both in the body and in the mind—quite the contrary of feeling sick and in pain, they experience a pleasurable stimulation.

The intellectual understanding of *pain of death* from smoking is dissonant with the feelings of pleasure experienced during the act of smoking. The tension produced by these contradictory ideas and experiences causes the smoker to find ways of rationalizing the conflict between the intellectual concept of pain and the physical experience of pleasure: smokers conclude things like "everyone dies in the end" or "smoking keeps me from gaining weight, which is also unhealthy" or "I'll just have one last one and then I'll give it up!" in order for the physical experience to rationally take precedence.

Because a physical experience is often stronger than an intellectual one for the human brain, dissonance becomes a threat to our self-concept (the knowledge we possess regarding ourselves, which creates our own, most stable idea of exactly who we are), and so the intellectual facts are rationalized into an alignment with the physical experience; the smoker has faith that he is not dying from smoking right now.

Illogic Can Be Rationalized

Excuses are always easier than behavioral change. Everybody from the bottom floor of an organization to the very top is prone to rationalizing conflicts in an effort to align what she is hearing with the perceived fact, truth, and reality of what she may see communicated. All of us are constantly rearranging, reinterpreting, or simply creating things that have been said in order to fit them into the world that we see in front of us.

Body Language Creates Illusions

I have always been fascinated by the natural world and the way it communicates, but my personal interest in (some would say obsession with) body language, nonverbal communication and persuasion and influence came from my fascination with illusionary mime as a young boy. I was highly entertained by those performers who could create the impression of walking in the wind, being lifted by a helium balloon and of course the much mocked "trapped in a glass box." I was totally engaged by their physical control and how it not only afforded them to tell a story without opening their mouths, but also changed their audience's perception of "reality." It was wonderful magic that looked and felt both fun and powerful, and so I put aside my initial desire for the life of a marine biologist, exchanged my hero Jacques Cousteau for Marcel Marceau, and spent hours practicing how to create these illusions myself for others.

Thus, it is so easy, once we have become assured that what we see is the truth, to continue seeing it as so even when there is strong evidence to the contrary through other channels—and so we come back to faith. And while beliefs are hard to undo, faith can often be blind and is therefore dangerous to the survival of any business. As the modern evolutionary biologist Richard Dawkins states, "Blind faith secures its own perpetuation by the simple unconscious expedient of discouraging rational inquiry."

This is why congruence between the verbal and the nonverbal is essential to the business communicator. Without a clear, consistent message conveyed on the two fronts of what we hear and what we see, a chasm of irrational thoughts opens up, potentially leading to some leaps of faith in the receiver that could produce some doomed outcomes.

Auditory Distortion

Again, with our hypothetical CFO's speech: if the verbal says, "It's been a great year!" and yet we see a physicality that suggests just the opposite—that there is no cause for celebration, and therefore perhaps no real financial gain—then we might create an auditory hallucination that causes the verbal content to fit the nonverbal attitude we are perceiving, and hear that "It's *not* been a great year."

But let's even just imagine that we have some prior knowledge from the company's financial auditors that it has indeed been a *great* year, and what is more, the dividend check we received in the mail that morning from our shares in the company was a fat one. If the nonverbal suggests that it has been a lousy year and cognitive dissonance occurs between what we know and what we see and believe, then we are quite likely to rationalize the incongruity. "Oh no—perhaps the next check will turn out to be no good!" Your stockbroker may advise you against selling, but that advice may fall on deaf ears because the broker did not *see* the speech you just heard. Your broker has only read the report and does not have the feeling you have about this company's fortunes. Your broker still has faith in the stock; you just lost yours.

The Eye of the Beholder

You're getting the picture, right? Unless an audience sees the right *image*, it doesn't hear the right *message*. The audience members may even make up their own message to fit the picture that they see, because the reality of this whole human communication system is that the receiver is ultimately in charge of the message received; it all gets translated in the receiver's head.

Sure, you may think you are sending out the message "*x*," but then you hear back that your audience heard the message "*y*." In order to minimize the possibility of this kind of total misinterpretation, you need to understand this:

The message happens in the audience's head.

The receiver is without doubt the most important person in any communication. Only by understanding this can you realize that you need to concentrate on not just the message that you send out, but also how it can potentially be interpreted. If you can concentrate on sending out nonverbal messages that are easy for the receiver to interpret correctly—clearly coded, with congruent images and sound—then the audience's brains stand a far greater chance of relaxing and getting your meaning in the way you intended.

To understand how your message could be interpreted and indeed misinterpreted, you will need to understand the mindset of your audience. You can then work toward shifting that mindset to one that *can* interpret your clear, congruent message in the way you intend. In order to understand your audience, you need to fix the following mantra in your mind every time you communicate:

It's not about me—it's about the audience.

Individual Interpretation

So much of the time in life in general, and particularly in business, it is easy to think that everything is about us. Well, of course! We are well practiced at creating the world around us in our own heads. The way the world exists to each of us personally is a creation resulting from the individual way in which our unique brains are specifically wired and patterned to receive the universe's messages. Our personal understanding of the world could be boiled down to the diversity of our individual genetic makeup, a result of experiences that have shaped our concepts about the world, or even a result of the noise that is getting between us and the message created in the environment in which we choose to be—in short, *nature, nurture,* and *choice.*

Because of this complex process of personal reception and creation, we constantly forget that every other person out there is also using his own individual process. Therefore, the world that we describe is not necessarily the exact world that others receive because of the way they are patterned to interpret our world in their minds. So we think we are communicating one thing, and yet we find out that it is perceived quite differently.

Of course, the usual business solution to this universal communication problem has been to create more and better content. You will recognize this as document obesity, PowerPoint overkill, lengthy speeches, and detailed discussions being held for hours "in the weeds" of the problem. This comes from a schoolroom mentality of getting high marks for demonstrating a high quantity of correct information. You have no doubt sat through laborious presentations and communications that take this attitude, and yet you know you were not engaged. The substance of the content is not what grabs audiences the most—it is the meaning that it has for us. However, you might instantly recognize this attitude as the one that you adopt when you are put on the spot: "We need *you* to make the presentation!" "Oh #@*%!—*What* am I going to *say!*"

They Need to Trust You

Remember, the members of your audience are just not that interested in you. This is not because they are selfish, but because they are human, sentient, and survivalist. They are watching you, and they need to experience a feeling of *trust* in what they see and hear from you first—for their own comfort. It is not what you say that builds that trust; it is what you do for them that allows them to feel it. As the American novelist Carl Buechner said, "They may forget what you said, but they will never forget how you made them feel."

Trust is the key to business. Indeed, Canadian Peter Munk, chairman and founder of Barrick Gold, the world's largest gold Mining Corporation, and one of the biggest entrepreneurs in mineral mining, has said, "The most important component to any business is trust."

Trust is a feeling, not a tangible thing. In the end, business deals do not come down to content; they come down to how much we trust the content—people buy *feelings*, not things! Help people to feel trust in you through your nonverbal communication, and whatever the substance of your content, it's going to get deep into their hearts and minds, and they are quite likely going to *do* whatever you ask!

In the end, it is what people *do* alongside you that will build the lasting connections between you. Shared experience of action is the glue for any group, tribe, or society. The greatest trust is built when people go beyond their individual survival, rise above the selfish gene, and advance to the evolutionary level of joining in "a movement" together. Group feeling through action is what affirms existence. **We act, therefore we are.**

So, by now you will want to know exactly what to do congruently with your body to win the trust of your audience. Of course you do, but first you must consider exactly what you have been doing incongruently in order to take on, install, and master these new physical techniques for good, and that is just what you'll do in the next chapter.

Chapter 1 Quick Study

We believe, trust, and act on what we see more than on anything else in the world. If we see something that does not fit exactly with what is being said, we feel that it is incongruent. We then trust what we saw as being the truth over what was said. This is not rational—but it is human. Great communicators are congruent and so cause less confusion or cognitive dissonance. Congruence in communication wins trust.

Just Do This Now

1. Which people in business do you trust and which do you not trust? Why do you not trust them? Have you witnessed them doing something that was not congruent in what they do and what they say and in line with what they had said or promised? Think how this makes you feel, and what would it take to get you to trust them again?

2. Ask yourself what you can *do* for people in business who may be losing trust in you.

3. Now see what happens if you take some immediate action to win back trust. How quickly do you see positive results for yourself and your business?

Chapter 1 Case Study

Theory to Practice: "Seeing" on a Screen?

"It really was strange to watch," explained the middle manager, describing the recent Webcast of the CEO's quarterly update. Trimmed budgets dictated that the "town hall meeting" of previous quarters was replaced by a "live Webcast" from the CEO's office, complete with real-time Q&A.

"From his speeches at all the other town halls, I would have described him as a great speaker and a very charismatic leader," she recounted. "That wasn't the case with the Webcast. I am not completely sure what the problem was. I can say that it had a negative effect on my view of his leadership and probably affected my involvement in achieving the vision."

With increased scrutiny of dollars spent, what are companies to do when the HR and corporate communications budgets do not allow these conference-type employee gatherings?

Insight

It is certainly worth asking questions like, "Do we really need to get everyone in the same place for these events?" The answer may continue to be yes because of the benefits derived from getting staff members "all fired up" over achieving the organization's goals.

The message could be identical, but look at the differences between the "broadcast" and "conference" events:

	Broadcast	Conference
Speaker frame	Sitting at a desk	Standing/moving on a stage
Audience surroundings	Sitting at my desk	In a large group in a hall
Interactivity	One-way visual and sound	Two-way visual and sound

In executing the broadcast option, presenters must address the incongruence of media presentation to effectively creating relatedness between leadership and staff and across the whole organization. Feelings of alienation and unrelatedness cause an avoidance response in the human mind and automatically turn us off to the content. Attention to body language should be a large part of the preparation for Web-enabled interactions such as the one just described. Being able to see more movement and body language that is more akin to a conference event can create more of a "group event" feeling by creating a more solid, human connection through the camera. To complete the experience, audience members can also form small or larger groups in their remote locations to watch the speech together.

Provocation

Why is it presumed that the physical language of business Webcasts should be like that of a studio news broadcast and not, say, that of a current affairs programme an outside broadcast, or even a prime-time game show—using the more entertaining and connected nonverbal style that goes with those genres?

If some of those potential styles don't feel businesslike to you, ask the questions, "What is entertainment," "What is business?" and "What would a body do to win at both of these?"

2

What We Have Here Is a Failure to Communicate

Shedding the Common Body Language of Bad Business

If we are strong, our strength will speak for itself.
If we are weak, words will be of no help.

—John F. Kennedy

In this chapter you'll learn:

- Why being an optimist is overrated
- How you're naturally hardwired for paranoia
- The chemistry of fear—and its mismanagement
- The biggest body language *don't* when presenting
- Top nonverbal ways to put an audience to sleep and lose business!

W hen we communicate, we are often unknowingly creating a potent feeling of distrust in others. Sadly, even established public speaking and presentation coaches worldwide consistently teach a common mistake that, more than any other factor, can overwhelmingly cause a speaker or business presenter to be viewed negatively by any audience. But before you learn how to never ever make that mistake yourself, and in so doing improve your mastery of nonverbal influence immediately, you must first understand this.

Why Have We Made It This Far?

There is a really good reason that you are looking at this page right now and reading these words, and it is not just that you want to improve your ability in human communication. You are right here, right now, alive and reading this because your brain has a very special way of thinking that naturally increases your chances of survival, and you inherited this routine process the very moment you were conceived. It is also responsible for the vast majority of the negative body language in business today.

So, let me give you the simple unconscious thought process that is naturally hardwired into your brain that helps to deliver you from potential threats:

First and foremost, take a negative view.

Optimists Are Frequently Surprised

Here is the way in which this preexisting programming works to your advantage. Imagine that you are an early human around about 200,000 years ago. It is the dead of night, and you are comfortable in your warm cave, asleep with your small family unit. Suddenly, your prehistoric partner wakes you up with a start and indicates that she has heard an ominous noise outside the cave entrance.

You are mentally predisposed to take the negative view, to instantly react *pessimistically*— "Uh-oh! It's a wildcat!"—and without blinking you quickly rouse the group, pick up the big stick that is lying next to you and move cautiously to the exit of your cave to potentially flee or defend yourself and your family from attack and possible death.

Now, it could indeed be a vicious animal, or it could just be the wind. If it is the first, you and your family stand a better chance of survival because *you are ready* and able to run or defend yourself and your genetic line as best you can; you were wise to be immediately and unconsciously wary, or pessimistic about the unknown sound. If it turns out to be only the wind in the trees, then you have lost nothing but a little sleep, but you have gained a statistically better chance of survival than, say, the prehistoric optimist, who in this selfsame situation thinks, "I bet it's nothing," and rolls over and goes back to sleep.

The optimistic mindset lets the person sleep soundly, but quite significantly lowers the chances of his genetic line surviving! The optimistic outlook leaves the sleeper unprepared to defend himself and his family should the chances that it's a predator go against him. So you can quite see how in a dog-eat-dog— or rather a large cat–eat-human—world, the optimists and their families were all soon dinner and the pessimists reproduced and survived.

The optimistic mindset has mostly been ironed out of our unconscious mind over time by the evolutionary process of natural selection. Darwinism at a neurological level has made the optimistic unconscious, for the most part, very nearly extinct. Only the programming for pessimism has predominantly survived within the unconscious mind. As we already know, it is that unconscious mind that rules our life on a daily basis, often for the sake of our personal survival and that of our species.

A Leopard Can't Change Its Spots

Now, think of all those colleagues, bosses, and gurus over the years who, when it comes to business communication, have advised you, "Hey, don't be so negative—be optimistic! Be positive! Once you get in front of the group, you'll be fine!" Upon closer examination, it turns out that they were expecting a leopard to change its spots, because in reality, our default mindset is *acutely paranoid*. Remember this, because you are going to discover later in this chapter just how the vast majority of communication and presentation training available to date ironically works fruitlessly against several million years of this natural survival programming. Being optimistic without being prepared dramatically increases the sense of unease in communicators and audiences alike by failing to recognize and respect how the mind and body fundamentally work when under pressure.

What's the proof? There is a plethora of communication/presentation training out there, and everyone in business seems to have attended course after course—yet we are all constantly bored, confused, disengaged, stupefied, and too often condescended to or even offended by the majority of what we see and hear. The bar on business communication is set so low that there are almost no entry-level requirements other than being a living human being (and even then some seem to have slipped through the net!). Statistics from Andy Lopata and Peter Roper's 2006 book on business communications, *And Death Came Third*, state that "81% of organizations were poor at presentation." According to many sources, giving a presentation is the number one fear in business, yet most organizations have naively instilled an optimistic cultural mindset concerning presenting.

Public Speaking Pessimism

All across the planet right now, leaders, entrepreneurs, and professionals of all kinds are stating their case in boardrooms, on stages, on TV, in meeting halls, in corridors, at networking meetings, and at lunches. And you can be sure that for the billions of people who are communicating under pressure right now, this simple, primeval routine programming of their unconscious minds to act on the *negative forecast* of any event is playing loudly in the background.

They come to present, and because there is very little hard information on how the communication will pan out for sure, positively or negatively, their ancient brain takes over and the primal pessimism kicks in to ensure their best chance of survival—or so it thinks.

You see, the primitive mind also sees everything in terms of black or white, good or bad—there is no gray area of thinking, no "maybe." If something looks potentially bad, then the primitive brain categorizes it as just *bad*, and the body's resulting reactions are those deemed appropriate by pre-organized response routines. Even anything that is unpredictable or uncertain will be categorized as a threat, in turn causing a retreat response—just to be safe and never sorry.

This means that presenters worldwide are in front of their audiences, thinking at a deep unconscious level, "There are other people here, and I don't know for sure what is going to happen, so I'll treat this as a threat—chances are that this will make me more likely to survive it." Of course, all they consciously experience is the feeling of "Oh, *@#!!!" Just like the prehistoric people of all our brains' pasts, the sympathetic nervous system, a control mechanism for our body's fundamental functions, initiates a response that is as familiar to us as it was to the first vertebrates on this planet—a response that can be traced back through our mammalian ancestors and reptiles, and right back to fish: *fight or flight*.

Danger When sensory data hit the brain stem, or, as some call it, the R complex or the reptilian brain, in a pattern that is registered and perceived as "danger," the rate of our adrenal activity is quickly increased. This, in turn, facilitates reliance on set behaviors that are often related to alertness, defense, and combat, along with the physical readiness to execute these tactics effectively—our fight-or-flight response is activated.

Also our simple reptilian mindset categorizes anything that we can't predict easily or is uncertain as a risk, and so stimulates our most fundamental nervous system to take in lots more data while closing down the number of categories to label and understand it by in order to allow quick computation and analysis. At the same time, our bodies fill up with adrenalin so that we can be physically ready for effective aggression toward the threat if running in the opposite direction has proved ineffective.

Presentation Anxiety

No surprise that business communicators at all levels often end up talking to their audiences in a frozen state, or one of submission or aggression. Their unconscious minds assume that they are not able to predict with any great certainty the exact outcome of this most critical and complex of human interactions. The more humans there are in the mix and the more imperative a positive outcome is, the more unpredictable and uncertain the situation appears to be to the unconscious mind. Complexity and importance bring about the unconscious imagination of a whole heap of possible threats and potential disappointments.

A presenter just has to get up in front of a group of people (any more than four is categorized as "many" by the unconscious mind), and in kicks the impulse to freeze, flee, fight, or finally *faint*—the "play dead" response. All of these begin by sending adrenalin coursing through the bloodstream, rapidly preparing the body for reaction and appropriate action in an immediate emergency situation. (In fact, even just one person can push the presenter's *unpredictability* button—"Will this person like my pitch or not?")

Acute anxiety—the result of all this stress—can eventually stimulate the release of a chemical called norepinephrine into the brain. This is the body's own antidepressant. (You'll recognize this as the high you feel when you finally get off the white-knuckle ride to make up for the terror you felt when you were on it, or the elated over-confidence of a poor presenter after a car crash of a corporate communication.) Further symptoms that you may recognize in others include a panic attack, a drained complexion, extreme fluctuations in temperature, sweating, dryness of the mouth and choking sensations, dizziness, feelings of "unreality" and confusion, introspection, and loss of concentration and memory.

These reactions are all a perfectly reasonable response to being attacked by a hungry lion; perhaps, however, rationally they could be considered a little over the top for reading from a PowerPoint slide in front of a small committee.

Animal Instinct

So presenters are freezing, fleeing, or fighting their audiences in fright (and maybe even feinting too, or at least taking a sick day) because they cannot safely predict the outcome of an important communication exchange. And how can we tell that the majority of them are doing this as they speak? Next time you are watching a series of business presentations, watch the presenters closely. Do you see their hands down by their sides, their stomachs crunched in, and their shoulders down (hunched over), chin tucked in, forehead down and eyes narrowed? Do you see some repetitive movement from side to side? This is the human body getting ready either to avoid attack, to be attacked, or to attack. And this is unfortunately how the vast, vast majority of business communicators meet their audiences to a lesser or greater degree.

What exactly is happening here? This posture drops the person's center of gravity to facilitate balance and power when ducking and running, to absorb the energy of an attack, or to spring into offensive action. The hands are below the waist to facilitate movement, as the arms are needed as pendulumlike weights (to walk or run, we need the swinging motion of our arms to help move us forward) to propel the body away from or toward a threat. The stomach is crunched in to shield the soft vital organs in that area, protected only by a muscle wall because of the body's design, which allows a diverse range of movement at the body's center (instead of protecting the core with skeletal tissue and suppressing mobility). Along with the repetitive shifting of weight to remain a moving target and the tucked-in chin to protect both the trachea and carotid artery, supplying oxygen to the body and blood to the brain and head down with narrowed eyes to protect sight, this is the posture of someone who is tremendously frightened or potentially highly aggressive.

Can you recall the last time *you* had something of a similar posture when you made a presentation?

View to a Kill

So it is the vulnerable "vital" or "kill" points of the body that we unconsciously protect when we feel anxious. The human race's business culture has introduced the format of "giving presentations" as a positive commercial tool, yet our old brains can't recognize the personal benefit. When we get up there to present, we still feel that age-old fear of danger. So we protect ourselves with posture. Furthermore, we will angle ourselves side on to the audience to decrease the vulnerable surface area to attack, or maybe hide a little behind an object such as a podium, chair, or table, touching this object for security and positioning ourselves in relation to it as we would to a shield or a weapon. We can also unconsciously gravitate toward windows and doors to be sure that we are close to an exit. Watch this behavior the next time you attend a presentation. More important, watch this behavior in yourself—it is natural, and you are predisposed to it. First recognize it, then, as you will find, you will be able to change it with the specific physical techniques coming up in the next chapter of this book.

Most important, how do you feel about the speaker when she presents to you in this way? Do you have confidence in her? Do you trust her? Do you feel that she is calm and assertive and able to deal with pressure as a leader? Is she credible to you as a potential provider? Or is she creating a feeling of distrust in you because what you see is someone who is showing all the fundamental signs of attack or retreat?

Think about the hypothetical scenario of our CFO telling us, "It's been a great year!": it may be this fight-or-flight posturing that is responsible for the incongruent nonverbal signals—the mixed messages that cause us not to trust the statement because of the physical impression that the CFO is prepping to flee or attack, is "stuck in the headlights," or is just rolling over and dying in front of us!

Pack Mentality

What's more, the pack copies the leader. The audience copies the presenter. Part of our brain is free of any logical thought process and is more emotionally based. It is sympathetic at an unconscious level with strong signals that it receives when watching and listening to other human beings. Not only do we have more faith in what we see, but we also have more faith in what we feel emotionally. Therefore, when we "connect" with another person on an emotional level, we trust the feelings that are communicated because they feel like they are *ours* too. We "mirror" or copy others' actions and feelings and have faith in them through our own physical and emotional experience of them.

It is theorized that the chemical that is most responsible for emotional bonding in humans, oxytocin, is involved in the human mirroring system, producing increased empathy and rapport and influencing generosity within partnerships and social groups. This chemical instills trust, increases loyalty, and promotes the "tend and befriend" response by diminishing fear—a response that is great for business in *so* many ways. When human beings get together, they can often display a complex and rapid exchange of largely nonverbal information regarding their emotional states. In other words, we can detect what others are feeling and rapidly adjust our own thinking, feeling, physiology, and actions to precisely match the situation. Part of your mind works alongside the sympathetic nervous system to release oxytocin for a deep, personal connection below the level of consciousness. It draws the emotions of a group into congruence. Human beings at all ages are active in this sense.

It is this reaction that causes any audience to mirror or mimic the messages that a presenter sends nonverbally. And in the case of the presenter displaying the symptom of fight or flight—well, the audience members just join right in. Only there are normally more of them than the speaker, so this can quickly spiral into a feedback loop of fear, aggression, and submission. *"Tough crowd. . . . I got eaten alive!"*

Mimic

Training in physical and visual theater opened up a huge vocabulary of movement for me, and I found that I was adept. I ate, drank, and slept the world of performance, and my eyes were opened to the extreme power in the body to understand and change psychological and emotional states. (More so than thought, intention and feeling can ever do by themselves.) Take, for example, the exercise of "pastiche," in which I would mimic another's personal movement rhythms and idiosyncratic gestures. This was most exciting when, in performing the other person, I could gain insights into her innate mindset through being receptive to the thoughts and feelings that copying her movement induced in me. One piece of vocabulary I would use when studying an individual was to discern whether he was "above the table" or "below the table"; this referred to the "TablePlane," (see Appendix) an imaginary surface that cuts through the body horizontally at the navel. If you take your center of gravity below that plane, you become sluggish, heavy, and often a little depressed in feeling—quite "passive." If you take your center of gravity above it, you became lighter, more airy, and a little more nimble mentally—quite "active." I would also see whether people were in front of the "door frame" or behind it. By imagining a surface that cuts through the body laterally and stepping your center of gravity either forward of this or behind it, you become psychologically more extroverted or introverted respectively. It is possible to go so far behind the door frame that you become so self-conscious that it is impossible for you to speak; you can also see this in others and shift them physically to give them instant confidence. By using combinations of these positions, one can literally step into another mental state while still being "authentic" because it is you doing it and so it is your genuine emotional state in that moment. For example, above the table and in front of the door frame can become hyper and aggressive—totally "in your face!" Try it out next time you want to clear a room quickly.

The Big Don't: Dropping Your Hands

Not only are you predisposed to drop your hands down by your sides when you present, *but the majority of traditional and present business presentation training tells you to do this!* These presentation manuals and trainers not only tell you to keep your hands loose by your sides, but also tell you to stand still. Let me make this quite clear: *you cannot do anything worse!*

Dropping your hands and standing still in front of an audience causes your unconscious mind to wonder why you have made yourself a static target. At this stage, your body will most likely respond by "playing dead." This is the mechanism that says that *if we are in danger and we are not going to move, we had better pretend to be very weak or even dead so that we don't get eaten.* That's when you get the weak body, dull voice, and, worst of all, a lifeless look in the eyes. The audience will see you as roadkill—highly unappetizing! This fright response can also lead to an almost narcoleptic sleep response or cataplexy (a muscular weakness brought on by strong emotion)—a feint response in the most acute cases of a stress response to public speaking.

The GrotesquePlane

I call the region of the body below the waistline the *GrotesquePlane*. (*Grotesque* comes from the same Latin root as *grotto*, meaning a small cave or hollow.) In modern English, grotesque has come to be used as a general adjective for something ugly, incongruous, or unpleasant, and thus it is often used to describe distorted forms. Not only this, but a cave is associated with dark, covert, and untrustworthy areas, where much is hidden from sight. The cave is where our prehistoric ancestors, and thus our animalistic instincts, live. Actioning gestures in the GrotesquePlane can open up the darker recesses of our instinctual mind. It is for these reasons that gestures in this area are so apt to be described as "in the grotesque."

Embodied Cognition

Let's now go through exactly what dropping your arms does to your body and your mind. In nature, there are really only two reasons for you to drop your arms: to rest or to move. We have talked about how with your arms dropped and your adrenalin pumping, you will start to shift your weight in front of an audience, literally looking shifty—not easy for those who are watching you to trust. This shifting can easily escalate to pacing up and down. The brain says that if we have our arms by our sides, we should be moving—especially with all those people looking at and judging us.

But when you stand still with your arms hanging down, the body takes this as a signal to rest, or even sleep. Yes, that's the biggest reason why the audience gets sleepy in a presentation: you are standing still with your arms hanging down. The audience members quickly copy the leader and let their arms relax in their chairs, sit back, and trance out. They become the living dead, just like the presenter. With the arms hanging down and the body still, a person's heart rate, breathing rate, blood pressure and levels of oxygen to the body and brain can decline quite rapidly taking the brain's electrical activity to a state that is getting dangerously near to the theta wave rhythmic cycle of sleep.

When the arms hang down and the body is still, the voice follows and drops significantly in tone (another nonverbal indicator of the meaning behind a message). This deeper voice then tends to drop even further at the end of each thought. Sighs and "ers" have a downward intonation, and there are really only three reasons for a downward intonation: sleep, depression, and command—the dormant presenter, the despondent speaker, and the despotic leader.

The Dormant Presenter If you wish to send a child to sleep with a story, just send the tone of your voice down at the end of each line of text, and start the next line at the deep tone you ended the last one on. So your voice drops down and down like a flight of stairs. The tone of voice informs the old brain that it is time to relax the body and decrease the breathing rate, heart rate, blood pressure and brain's activity. Certain chemicals are sent around the body to tell the brain to start shutting down some of the nonvital functions, most importantly the conscious mind. The child's skin begins to go paler and waxy in tone as his eyes begin to glaze over and his limbs begin to go limp. You see, it is not the story that sends us to sleep, but the tonality of the reading that gives us the instruction at a deep, deep level.

And you have certainly witnessed speakers and presenters who have put both themselves and their audience to sleep in seconds with their downward-inflected tonality. Putting the hands down by the sides and being still is the culprit that is largely responsible for this tranquilizing tonality.

The Despondent Presenter Next is the depressed downward tonality—the chief financial officer who tells us, "It's been a great year!" but in a tonality that says, "I am close to hanging myself. . . . Dump my stock right now." As Dr. Mehrabian's studies concluded, given a choice between believing the content and believing the nonverbal messages, the unconscious mind will go with the nonverbal as being more trustworthy. Once again, hands down by the sides is a sure-fire route to creating a downturn in credibility.

The Despotic Presenter Finally, there is the loud-voiced downward tonality, which is more prone to happen when the hands are down at the sides and the body is pacing. Pacing up and down in the space creates the over-confidence of being a moving target and puts more air into the lungs; the brain functions better with more oxygen intake and processes some of the fight-or-flight chemicals so as not to depress and poison the system. However the extra air volume in the lungs gives a loud, forceful downward inflection that can sound overtly commanding, especially when mixed with an adrenalin fueled attitude — a product of the aggressive "fight" response. This may be acceptable to an audience that feels that it is clearly under threat from somewhere else and can sense that dangerous uncertainty personally; such people will be attracted to a strong command structure in the tone of the voice. It will feel more certain and so safer to them. More often than not, however, in the modern business world the commanding voice seems too aggressive and often just crazy. Trust disappears because the audience members cannot see for themselves the imminent threat to which the leader seems to be having a strong response.

Armed forces use the command tonality to great effect in training to stop the soldiers from questioning what the threat is when they cannot see it. It can take months of repetitive drill and other "incentives" to *emotionally desensitize* combatants so that they will respond to orders without question in all circumstances, obeying commands during periods of stress or when they are under no perceived stress.

To illustrate, consider a military combat situation. When a soldier encounters an initial sign of threat, the socially appropriate response, i.e., the response demanded by his military training and reinforced by other members of his unit, is usually the "stop, watch, and listen" heightened-alertness response. This behavior is consistent with the biological predisposition toward the freeze response. But as the reality of a firefight grows imminent, the biological and situational demands are no longer so aligned. The evolved hardwired instinctual response to flee is in conflict with military training, and this conflict can further increase the intensity of this already stressful experience. This is why the military has some unique and highly effective training methods to manage and desensitize soldiers to operation stress and counteract their natural instincts to flight rather than fight. However, these training techniques are frankly a little extreme for the business communicator's needs. We will leave them well alone.

For most of us who are neither giving nor receiving military orders, in our daily business dealings, barking commands can often kill rapport and get you a name for being an insensitive idiot, potentially quashing lucrative deals in your wake. "I love the smell of napalm in the boardroom!"

Lead with Your Body

Given this new insight, if you have any publications or training manuals that tell you to keep your hands by your sides when you speak, do yourself a favor now, and tear those pages out and burn them! Indeed, burn the whole book or training manual, because if that is some of its best advice, what is its worst like?

What these trainers do not know is the fundamental effect of certain movements on the brains of both the person who is moving and anyone viewing that movement. They have no knowledge of the powerful effect that even small movements of the body have on the emotional impulses of the mind. Of course, masters of the performing arts have known these secrets for thousands of years, and more recently behavioral psychologists and neurologists have recognized the significance of the motor system in influencing cognitive and affective processes. As George Lakoff, a champion of theories on embodied cognition, states in his 2002 work *Moral Politics,* "Our brains take their input from the rest of our bodies. What our bodies are like and how they function in the world thus structures the very concepts we can use to think. We cannot think just anything—only what our embodied brains permit."

Specific movements may become so strongly associated with a cognitive or affective state that their initiation consistently elicits that corresponding state. As the simplest example, take the way arm flexion is habitually used for pulling something toward oneself, and arm extension for pushing something away. As a result, these movements have become associated with positive and negative outcomes, respectively, and psychological researchers have proven that performing them tends to invoke corresponding reactions. For instance, conscious use of such approach and repel arm movements can influence an individuals' feelings of liking or dislike respectively.

His Master's Voice

Movement experts such as the world-renowned Moshé Feldenkrais (physicist, World War II spy, judo expert and teacher at the Esalen Institute), in his book *Awareness through Movement* (1972), recognize that since the nervous system is mainly occupied with movement, "Correction of movement is the best means of self improvement." As in the European schools of acting stemming from Michael Chekhov and the modern American methods from Sanford Meisner, the idea of "impulse" is key to creating "authentic" performance. Spontaneous instinct drives human behavior, and so emotional impulses and not sense memory or emotional memory inform the most dynamic of acting techniques. Authentic feelings arise from activities and reactions to "the moment" or "the now." This is fundamentally why actors are called actors—they *do* action. If thinking where of primary importance in the moment of performance they would be called philosophers. Not only this, but as Europe's foremost mask theater acting expert John Wright puts it, "That same impulse can be sustained and have influence on the voice."

The world's greatest vocal performance teachers, such as Frankie Armstrong, Cicily Berry, and Patsy Rodenberg, concur that the body and the voice are inextricably linked. For the average business professional, this means that body language works not only when the audience can see you, but even when it can't! Because even a subtle physical impulse affects the vocal muscles to such a strong degree, when you use body language over the telephone, your audience can hear your intention more clearly when you concentrate on physically projecting that intention rather than merely intending it psychologically. As one great acting trainer was often heard to say to students "you are boring me—an audience cannot hear or see you thinking however hard you are doing it, you must show them."

Of course, if you are not aware of any negative body language when you talk over the telephone, you will be equally unaware of the negative tonality that your audience is hearing from you.

What Did I Tell You

This book is a unique combination of ancient secrets and new science, so remember that I said, "If at any moment you begin to feel like questioning a technique or its rationale—step backward, take a breath, *trust*, and just do it!" Understand that literally *stepping backward* (a traditional method for taking stock and thinking about a situation) has been shown in psychological tests to significantly enhance cognitive performance in moments of stress (this avoidance pattern of movement decreases anxiety). Indeed backward motion appears to be a very powerful trigger to mobilize cognitive resources. In fact, it was found conclusively in tests at Radboud University, Netherlands, in 2008 that whenever you encounter a difficult mental situation, stepping backward may boost your capability to deal with it effectively.

We will look at exactly what taking a breath can do for you and your business audience in a further chapter—but first, if you would like to know and master the secret of *exactly where* to place your hands in order to take countermeasures to calm your fight-or-flight response system, and instantly win a feeling of trust from your audience, then read on.

Chapter 2 Quick Study

The GrotesqueGesturePlane: When you drop your hands down by your sides in a stressful situation, your body is designed to execute its extreme stress response. Your audience is prone to mirror or copy this response and feel uneasy, confused, or sleepy. Since for the majority of businesspeople, communication is their biggest problem and often has the most impact on relationships and on business, it is best, when communicating, to avoid doing anything that can exacerbate the fear of speaking. And some business content being just plain boring (sorry, but it is)—it's best not to encourage sleep.

Just Do This Now

1. Keep your hands above your waistline (see next chapter for specifics) and so out of the GrotesquePlane when you communicate to avoid negative engagement with your audience.

2. Should you wish to lower the energy of your audience (maybe they are too excited), let your hands drop down by your sides and stand still.

3. Allow your voice to follow the impulse of your body to reduce strain on it. Let your voice do what it naturally wants to do in alignment with your chosen physicality.

Chapter 2 Case Study

Theory to Practice: Literally Breathtaking

In a seventh-grade classroom, Mr. Williams interrupts John's public speaking delivery as John becomes faint. On the verge of collapse from lack of oxygen, John takes an empty front-row seat. His friend David soon escorts him to the bathroom.

In a project update, Shawn's speech begins to slow and a slight gasp/swallow motion begins to pepper his presentation with alarming frequency. He reduces the "Key Take-Away" portion of his talk to simply reading the bullet points on the presentation slide. He regains his composure after stumbling through an answer to the first audience question looking for clarification on much of the content.

In both cases, audience members are aware that something is amiss, and are completely distracted from the presentation. Nobody says anything, and there is limited positive discussion following the episode.

Insight

Certain body positions send clear messages that start some quite extreme physiological and psychological responses. What was just described is a natural—and relatively frequent—occurrence when people address groups (e.g., more than four other people). It is very likely that both these presenters stood still, kept their hands in the GrotesquePlane and literally starved their brains of oxygen.

Provocation

In seventh grade, the teacher can come to your aid. What kind of impression are you making in the workplace when this happens?

3

Winning Trust with a Wave of Your Hand

Truth Fears No Question

Life happens at the level of events. Trust only movement.

—Alfred Adler

In this chapter you'll learn:

- The TruthPlane and how to be there
- The world's top technique for using the body to win trust
- The biggest key to nonverbal excellence
- How to calm stage fright—with your hands
- Ancient techniques for talking to the reptilian brain

If you were not feeling confident about your standing in a social group, you would not wish to show this vulnerability on purpose, would you? If you felt weak and exposed around a group, you would not go out of your way to display that weakness and expose yourself more, right? In the body language you use in a business context, the last thing you might think it wise to do is to expose and display your own Achilles' heel. It seems as though you are better off putting on a mask of boldly assertive body language that shows that *you are strong*—the alpha person in the room, with an air of invincibility, yes?

No!

You are about to learn the key piece of nonverbal communication that is understood in every culture around the world and shows that you are non-confrontational, open, available, and accepting of others. Some of you will be thinking, "Well, that's a weak strategy," but you'd be quite wrong. The people in any business audience—at a presentation or a meeting, or standing around the water cooler for a chat—are not looking for someone who is going to harm them—they are looking for someone who is going to *help* them. They need to feel sure that the leader in the room is going to give them sustenance, not deplete their resources. Most of all, they must be assured that you *accept* them. If you look as if you will "feed them," they will approach you. If you look as if you are going to "take away," then they will retreat or attack.

The Gesture That Time Forgot

The following simple piece of body language, hundreds of thousands of years old and still applicable today, is totally overlooked in understanding by nonverbal communication "experts" and business presentation trainers around the globe. It has, however, been handed down within the community of visual communicators for centuries. Until this point, it has never been put into writing for any business audience, with any full explanation of its powerful properties.

So here is that signal that instantly lets the members of an audience know that you are genuine in intention and can be trusted:

Gestures on a horizontal plane extending from the navel.

OK, so what you may be thinking now is, *it can't be that simple!* Yet, as you are about to experience and learn for yourself, it really is. All you have to do to let the audience know that you are here to give rather than to take away is to make hand gestures along the horizontal plane from your navel, because what those gestures are is not as important as *where* they are when it comes to showing your honest intentions toward others. So let's do some practical work to help you understand and experience the incredibly influential and persuasive powers of working within this gesture position, which I have named the *TruthPlane*.

Hands-On

First if you stand tall and upright now but allow your hands to hang down by your sides (below the waistline) in the *GrotesquePlane* of gesture you should start to pay attention to your breathing rate. Note the pace and the quality of the breaths in and out that you are taking. For example, is your breathing slow-paced, fast-paced, or what you might describe as mid-paced? Do you feel as if you are taking in deep breaths, shallow breaths, or something you might describe as somewhere in between the two? Do you feel that you are *taking in* more breath than you are *breathing out*, or vice versa, that you are breathing out more air than you are breathing in?

As you stand, notice some details of your physical stance as a whole when your arms are hanging down on each side of your torso. How stable are your legs? How erect is your spine? How does your head feel right now on the top of your neck? How does your face feel? What are the muscles in your face doing, and what do you think is the nature of the expression of your mouth, your eyes, your forehead, and across your face as a whole?

In addition to this, how do you *feel* right now? Describe that feeling to yourself, or even name it if you can. Many people get a considerable feeling of "heaviness" in the physical, mental, and emotional sense. Consider whether that is what you are feeling as well. Finally, note anything you experience beyond that which has been outlined, and remember it all for comparison later.

TruthPlane

Again, tall and upright, but now bring your hands up to your belly button, and just gently interlace the fingers of your left and right hands so that they are held comfortably and lightly over your navel, with your palms softly touching your stomach.

Can you immediately feel a difference in the way you are breathing? Is your breathing faster or slower than before? Has your breathing become deeper or shallower, or even perhaps more balanced? Do you feel that you are breathing out more than you are breathing in, or is there a sense of equilibrium to your breathing? How does your breathing generally compare to the breathing that you experienced with your arms hanging at your sides? Note the difference for yourself right now.

Bring your attention to your body as a whole. How are you standing right now? For example, how secure do you now feel in your feet and legs? How does this compare to your stance in the GrotesquePlane of gesture? What do you feel and think about the position of your spine and how your head now sits on your neck? Can you feel a difference, and if so, what makes up that important difference for you?

Again, pay attention to your face. How do the muscles around your mouth, eyes, and forehead feel to you? What is the expression that you now feel that you have, and what is the feeling that goes with that expression on your face? Can you describe the feeling that having your hands gently in the plane extending from your navel gives you, and can you give that feeling a name? Also take note of anything else that you have experienced or thought since taking up this second position of the hands, especially in relation to your earlier experience of the GrotesquePlane.

Quickly drop your hands down by your sides into the GrotesquePlane or keep the fingers interlaced so that your hands fall in front of your groin. How fast do you revert to the original breathing pattern, stance, positioning, and feelings that go with this position? Now bring your hands up to your navel area and allow them to gesture anywhere in horizontal plane that extends 180° from a centre that is your navel. Be open with your gesture, giving clear access to the stomach. How quickly does the feeling that goes with the new physical position change?

The Result? A Feeling of Calm

Many people describe the feeling that they get from having their hands in the navel or belly-button area as being "centered," "controlled," "collected," "composed," or "calm" (generally a lot of things beginning with the letter *c*); but also, just as you will have experienced, they get a sensation of levelheadedness, balance, and abundant energy.

Why do we get a feeling of security and calm when we place our hands in this navel area, bringing attention and access to it as opposed to the feeling of lethargy, apathy, and sometimes aggression that comes when our hands are hanging in the GrotesquePlane—either to the sides, across our front or clasped together around the back? To answer this, let's first look at what centuries-old Eastern thought tells us about this area of the body.

Red Mercury In traditional Chinese medicine and martial arts, the area just a couple of fingers width below the belly button is known as the lower *dantien*, which translates loosely as "red field" and is a storage center and powerhouse for pure energy. Also, and for the purposes of understanding the physical importance of this area and its initial relevance to nonverbal communication, the lower *dantien* is taken as roughly the point where the sagittal, coronal and transverse planes of the human body intersect, or "the one point." In Chinese and Japanese tradition (along with much Western sports practice), this is considered the physical center of gravity for the human body. (See Appendix)

Scientific theories and practices about centers of gravity, formed first by the famous Greek physicist Archimedes in the second century BC, state that in any system of particles, there is a specific location at which the whole system's mass behaves as if it were concentrated, and so the center of mass is the point at which the whole of a body can be acted upon by gravity. Therefore, if you act upon a body's center of mass, you are very likely to act upon that whole body. The most productive input of energy to affect any mass is at its center.

Control the Center to Control the Whole

Recognize as well that the center of mass within a body does not always coincide with its geometric center. With our human center of mass, by manipulating the shape of our body, we can shift the center of gravity to different parts of the body or even outside of it. And this property can be exploited. When an Olympic high jumper performs a "Fosbury flop," he bends his body in such a way that it is possible for the center of mass to shift along the body so as to allow parts of the jumper's body to be relieved of the center of gravity in order to clear the bar with more ease.

So it is in the area of our navel, or belly button, that we have the most balanced center of gravity when we are standing still on firm ground. This is the primary reason for the feeling of physical stability that is produced when you stand with your hands anywhere on a plane extending from that belly-button region of the body: you are aligning more of your mass with the center of that horizontal plane.

Plane Truth

I first came across the horizontal planes of gesture and their effect on the psychology of an audience when I was training in the art of mask performance, demonstrating the effects of these GesturePlanes to audiences. Under the instruction of my teacher and mentor, John Wright, I would take some very simple pieces of text and demonstrate to an audience the profound effects that delivering these words with the hands at different horizontal levels had in changing both the way the words "felt" to me as I said them and the resulting effect on the audience that was hearing and seeing them. The results could be anything from breathtakingly profound to hilariously funny, depending on the congruence between the standard linguistic meaning of words and intention found within the corresponding GesturePlane used. No matter what the result from the audience, it was based on a *fundamental and innate understanding of the sincerity of the gesture over the words*. Where this system originally came from is difficult to pin down (acting training being an experience and not a manual). I would predict that it may have been handed down orally through Jacques Copeau or his nephew Michel Saint-Denis to George Devine in the U.K., who collaborated with the likes of John Gielgud, Laurence Olivier, and Alec Guinness. (Devine worked with Saint-Denis on what eventually became the Old Vic Theatre School, a British icon housing legends of theater training through physicality such as Rudi Shelly, teaching well into his nineties, and creating actors such as Sir Patrick Stewart, Daniel Day-Lewis, and even Gene Wilder.) The work of Copeau and Saint-Denis had a profound effect on performing arts across the world, influencing Michael Chekhov and eventually Stanislavski who evolved his own ideas on "substitution of emotional memory" toward Chekov's more powerful more imaginative techniques of "The Method of Physical Action" and "Psychological Gesture," that have informed thousands of Hollywood actors today from Marilyn Monroe to Johnny Depp.

Breathing from the Stomach

The stomach is an important area of focus in business communication skills for reasons beyond gesturing. Breathing from the stomach is another great way to feel at ease during a presentation. Before any act or action, we need oxygen as fuel. It is no surprise that the belly button or navel area plays an important, even essential role in breathing techniques practiced all over the world, from the Qigong's "embryonic breathing" and storage of vital Chi energy to an Opera singer's powerful volume and range.

For example, in stage acting, "breathing from the belly"—controlling the muscles of the diaphragm—is an invaluable professional technique, the purpose of which is to draw air into the bottom portion of the lungs before the chest muscles expand and draw further air into the upper portion. This centuries-old trick of the trade dramatically increases lung capacity, and therefore the amount of oxygen available from each breath, allowing the stage actor the maximum vocal strength. Control of the diaphragm is also used to regulate the pressure and volume of air passed over the vocal cords, producing more consistent tone in the human voice.

And there is more convincing evidence for this technique's power in business communication: the *dantien* is linked directly with the adrenal glands— that area that is responsible for the extreme stress response of fight or flight described in Chapter 2 and as seen in the diagram of the major organs of the endocrine system in Figure 3.1. All these endocrine organs are instrumental in regulating metabolism, growth, development, and tissue function, and also play a most important role in determining mood and dealing with reactions to stress, such as the fight-or-flight response mechanism.

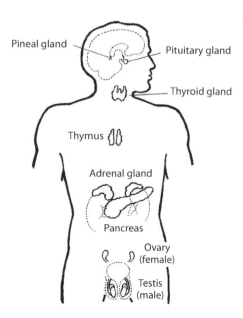

Figure 3.1 The Endocrine System

Navel Intelligence

The adrenal glands are situated (as their name indicates: *ad*, meaning "at," plus *renes*, meaning "kidneys") on top of the kidneys and in front of the twelfth thoracic vertebra. The adrenal glands are chiefly responsible for regulating stress responses from your hormones. These hormones all play a part in the fight-or-flight response activated by the sympathetic nervous system. In simple terms, the adrenal glands link the thoughts of the brain to physical action in the human body. They are pieces of primitive brain that, instead of thinking, just get down to chemically reacting when they are stimulated in the right way.

So, whether you, as a businessperson, want to also join in with the ancient beliefs of the East or not, it is pretty clear from a couple of hundred years of modern Western endocrinology that the navel is indeed the control center of your physical balance and the center of your biological mechanism for coping with stress (and you do get stressed!).

However you wish to look at it, the insight to take away from the unique discovery of the TruthPlane (Figure 3.2) and how the body affects the mind (embodied cognition) is this:

When the hands gesture within the TruthPlane, an energized calm, confident, and balanced effect is felt by both the communicator and the receiver.

Not only does having your hands in this position affect your body language, but it also affects your whole nonverbal presence. Because of the interconnected nature of the physical system, your vocal tone is affected congruently with the GesturePlane. Therefore, your whole vocal tone becomes more calming and trustworthy. This is another reason why this technique is so effective—it changes one's voice quite profoundly and with-

Figure 3.2 The TruthPlane

out the laborious vocal exercises that many other performance and presentation coaches recommend (and that you then forget to perform in the moment of crisis).

Exercise: Ordering Anxiety

Now it is time for you to try to experience the calm, confident, active effect of placing your hands within the TruthPlane while you are under conditions of stress. You are going to order a pizza! OK, you are thinking—what is so stressful about that? Well, here is the catch: you are going to walk into two stores, neither of which makes or sells pizza, or, indeed, any type of food or drink. A clothing store would be a good choice, or perhaps a bookstore. Because you know that entering a clothing store and asking the assistant for a pizza is potentially (if not definitely) embarrassing for you, this should cause your central nervous system to push your sympathetic nervous system into activating the stress-regulating system situated toward the back of your belly. Indeed, you should get a shot of adrenaline as you approach the store and certainly a shot as you approach the counter or the fashionable assistant with your food request.

For some of you, just imagining putting yourself in this situation will already be causing you to feel the adrenaline rush — that odd churning feeling in your stomach, dryness in your mouth, and the color draining from your face. So, for those of you who are unable to complete this exercise for whatever reason, you may try it in your imagination, because it may already be doing a great job of firing up your fight-or-flight response just as a thought exercise.

The GrotesquePlane

In the first store or shop, make sure that you have your hands down by your sides in the GrotesquePlane. Try to monitor the level of stress and anxiety that you feel, and take careful note of the type of response you get from the assistant. Note that some of you may not even make it into the store because of the high levels of fear this exercise provokes!

The TruthPlane

Now for the second store: place you hands anywhere within the horizontal plane that extends at the height of your belly button. Allow about three ordinary breaths in and out with your hands in this area to balance out the oxygen levels in your bloodstream and restore equilibrium, particularly in light of your experience in the first store (or your experience outside of the store, for those of you who are acting out the physical instructions solely in your imagination).

Walk right into the store and keep your hands gesturing anywhere in the TruthPlane as you approach the service counter or assistant. When you ask for help with a pizza, be sure to only gesture with your hands gesturing out from this horizontal plane. Keep your hands totally level on the horizontal plane that potentially spreads out a full 180° from the center point of your belly button and goes out and beyond your personal space. Pay close attention to how you now cope with this stressful situation (or your imagined stressful situation), and pay close attention to the effect you feel you are having on the assistant this time around.

Debrief

Now that you've done this exercise, how did it go? How did you feel the second time around when your hands were stabilized in the belly area, as opposed to hanging by your sides in the GrotesquePlane when you approached the first shop? Did you feel more in control of your breathing the second time around (either for real or in your imagined encounter)? Did you feel more control over your feelings of stress the second time around? Did you notice any calmer reactions from the person with whom you spoke? (I'm sure you may have an understanding by now that presenting the shop assistant with this moment of dissonance is extremely stressful for her, too.) Did you find that this very simple piece of body language made an enormous difference to the situation, not only in providing you with stable feelings of balance, breathing, and bravery, but also in the type of reaction you got? Did others pay more calm attention to you?

Tone

What did you notice about the nonverbal element of communication in the *tone of your voice* when you were gesturing in the TruthPlane? Did you notice, as others often do, the calm and gently upward-inflecting tone, as opposed to the downward intonation of the GrotesquePlane?

By now you will be starting to understand how making simple and clear decisions in the way you use your body language promotes clear decisions in the sound of your voice, along with clear decisions from others around you. You will also by now be getting the picture of how this simple idea of keeping your gestures within the TruthPlane affects how confident you feel and the confidence you display, not only in your body but in your voice. So let's look now at the most important factor in all of this: the effect that gesturing in the TruthPlane has on your audience.

Under the Influence

When you are under stress, you cannot stop your adrenal glands from doing their job because you cannot stop your brain stem from asking them to do their job—the process is involuntary. Your reptilian brain is not under your conscious control, especially in times of stress, when its purpose of saving your life really comes into its own. However, by physically keeping your gestures in the TruthPlane, you can effectively introduce a countermeasure to push back against the reaction in the R-complex part of your brain and in your adrenal glands. (Those of you who have tested this in the crazy pizza experiment should have real proof of this by now.)

And because you can now present this countermeasure to your natural reactions to stress, you enable the members of your audience to unconsciously mirror that countermeasure and reduce their stress along with you. Remember that the audience members are programmed at a deep level to copy. They are designed to copy the confidence that you portray nonverbally, and to frame any *verbal* message that you are delivering with your confident body and the tonality that naturally goes with it.

Placing your hands in the TruthPlane is *the* single most effective way for the business communicator to fight back effortlessly against the natural stress reaction and send out a clear signal to the audience that there is no problem, that everyone, including you, can be very confident. After all, why would you be displaying and drawing unconscious attention to this very vulnerable stomach area (both in terms of physical balance and unprotected vital organs) if you were under stress and, from your brain's point of view, "under attack"?

This is why not only do you feel more confident presenting yourself in this physical position, but others around you become more confident, too: they feel that you are confident, calm, stable and balanced, attentive, intelligent, and, most important, honest, authentic, and *trustworthy*. This is why this belly area is called the TruthPlane.

Taste Test

Here's a quick experiment: take a look at the two silhouettes in Figure 3.3 and ask yourself which person you trust more than the other.

Which of the two would you trust more when you heard the words, "It's been a great year for our company"?

It's interesting how, even with simple silhouettes, when the hands appear to be in the GrotesquePlane (the hands appear below the waistline) we the audience feel less assured and less trusting, compared with how we feel toward the silhouette with the hands at navel height.

Figure 3.3 The GrotesquePlane versus the TruthPlane

This is all due to your reptilian brain, which is designed to look at the simple body positioning and movement of another human being in order to make a very quick decision as to whether or not that person is a potential threat or a potential friend. Considering the pictures, it may seem illogical for you to rate the two pictures differently because, after all, they both seem to be lacking such a lot of clear information upon which to base a logical decision. But again notice how remarkably easy it is for your fast unconscious process to make a satisfactory decision as to which one you trust more, even though the figures are unclear and in black and white.

Trust Me, I'm A Spin Doctor

Of course, skilled persuaders throughout history have always known of the properties and effects of working with an audience from the TruthPlane. Figure 3.4 gives a classic physical pose from history that shows this.

Figure 3.4 Meditative Buddha

How could you not trust him? He's so very centered and calm sitting there. And it is not about the serenity in the face; if you cover the head with your hand, you will notice that you continue to perceive a feeling of confident stillness. Facial features are not initially as important as the bulk of the body mass, especially the positioning of the center of gravity and the hands, in how we all determine the intention and emotional state of another human being. Indeed, in a recent study by Dr. Anthony Atkins, it was found that a major part of emotional recognition as a prescreening device for social interaction comes from the body alone and excludes the face. Atkins states, "The way people move their bodies tells us a lot about their feelings or intentions and we use this information on a daily basis to communicate with each other."

Figure 3.5 shows another image where, again, although the figure is bent forward, the hands are within the TruthPlane.

It is difficult to imagine anything other than a genuine and well-intentioned action in this picture. Again, we certainly feel that we can trust this person. Of course, that sheds some light on why the artists who created these

Figure 3.5 Jesus Blesses the Children

images have chosen this physical positioning of the hands at the height of the belly and open; across all cultures and across all times, it is the strongest symbol for "you can trust me."

News Flash

And for more contemporary examples of the power of the TruthPlane, watch any TV reporter, presenter, or anchor who is delivering a piece of factual news; yes, that person's hands are in the TruthPlane. As professional communicators to a mass audience, many of these people unconsciously understand (or have been trained in the TruthPlane system) that if they place their hands at navel height, they will feel and sound more confident, and the viewers will feel confident with that anchor delivering the important "factual" information of the day. When people stand with their hands in the TruthPlane and deliver the story, we all start to feel that, for sure and certain, everything they are saying is factual. Yet we don't know why we're sure—we simply *trust* it based on the clear signal in body language and tone of voice as old as humankind that *this* human being (the reporter) is to be trusted, and therefore what he says is the truth.

Try It Right Now

You should begin to use this most important body language gesture to win trust immediately. Try it right now with your friends and colleagues. Notice your confidence; notice the clear, calm quality in your voice; and notice the positive attention that you get instantly. Notice others who do not use this plane of gesture when it would serve them well. Can you imagine how much better you would respond if they were presenting to you or having a business conversation with you from the TruthPlane? Decide right now how you are going to use this powerful secret of winning body language to your immediate business advantage today, and read on for much, much more.

Chapter 3 Quick Study

TruthPlane: The primal stress response experienced by both you and the receivers of your message when you communicate under pressure *can be counteracted* by placing your hands anywhere on the horizontal plane that extends out 180° from a center of the navel—or, as I call it, the Truth-Plane. Open gestures in the plane are the most effective way to engender trust with other humans in micro-seconds

Just Do This Now

1. When you communicate, place your hands as much as possible in the TruthPlane—the horizontal plane that extends out from the navel area (or in anatomical terms, at the "Transverse Plane" or "Axial Plane" that divides the body into cranial and caudal—head and tail—portions).
2. Use the TruthPlane to cause your body and mind to be calm during communications.
3. Lead your audience members to become confident in you and in themselves by placing your hands and gestures open in the TruthPlane when you communicate with them, framing their access to your vulnerable belly area and bringing unconscious attention to it (even over the telephone, because the impulse affects your voice in a profound way, too).

Chapter 3 Case Study

Theory to Practice: Cutting Corners

Flo is the alliance manager on a strategic partnership. In accordance with the contracts, she meets with her counterpart early in April to determine volume and pricing specifics for the fiscal year, which begins in July.

She is somewhat frustrated by the tension that seems to result from the conversations, which are always held on the client's "turf" in the same boardroom. Both sides know that they need to work together, and they always reach agreements that are within the anticipated range. Why does it have to feel so much like a negotiation?

Insight

The physical setup of a room can create an aggressive response that comes from your visual cues. Think of a typical boardroom scenario like this:

- The parties sit on opposite sides of the table.
- They lean forward slightly, thereby hiding their stomachs.
- Their hands may be hidden below the table at first.

This combination of body language elicits a defensive response from the limbic system. Flo could expect a vastly different—and more receptive—dynamic if she were to try to sit in a position (perhaps at a corner of the table) that puts less of a visual barrier between herself and her counterpart. This will foster more elements of communication from the TruthPlane with the middle section of her the body clearly visible.

Provocation

Why do we so often let the traditional organization of a room dictate our actions instead of controlling our environment and body to align with our objective?

4

Inspirational Influence out of Thin Air

Breathe In the Possibilities

*Breathe . . . and remind yourself that this very moment
is the only one you know you have for sure.*

—Oprah Winfrey

In this chapter, you'll learn:

- How to expand your senses when you are communicating
- When to conspire with your audience to influence and persuade
- The first step to being inspirational every time you speak
- A mistake that can kill you and your audience
- How to be imaginative—the easy way

Everyone wants to be an inspiration to others, but not all of us are famous or gregarious, life-of-the-party types; many of us are perhaps more behind-the-scenes folks. Regardless of how we individually operate in business or in society, however, the vast majority of us want to impress others with the help that we have to offer, and in such a way that others are compelled and inspired to act upon that help and perhaps even inspire others with it also. Some people call this a *legacy*.

We all leave behind something in every interaction that we have. Some people define this as an aspect of your personal *brand experience*—the impression that you have or leave on others. Every time you interact and communicate, you create and leave behind ripples in the ponds of a great many individual perceptions, emanating out across time and space from the point of the interaction. Well after you physically leave any one inter-action, the experience of your legacy lives on in the way others react to you, what they think and feel about you, what they are going to do with the message they have received from you, and to what extent they feel energized and inspired to work along with you.

There is simply no downside to effecting inspiration—so how great would it be to stand the best chance of inspiring the people around you every time you interact, and to be able to do this not with your words, but with your body? You know by now from reading the first few chapters that much of the time people trust the body and vocal quality (the nonverbal communication) over the words—a whole lot more than you may have pre-viously imagined.

Breath Control

We decide what type of person we are dealing with by what we see him or her do. This is the way we get a "feeling" for people. Some people appear to be wholly present and *alive* in front of us, and others . . . not so much. Knowing that all our judgments about the outside world are influenced by the feelings we have inside us (even the feeling that we are being rational), if we could change the way others feel, then we could change the way they judge us and everything we say and do in our business life.

That is why in this chapter you are going to learn and practice the biggest key to changing others' opinions of you, and their propensity to accept your messages—just by breathing! This chapter looks at the science of how *breath* changes brain function; the predominant breathing patterns in poor business body language; how to breathe in such a way that it makes you sharper and more positive, creative, and alive; how others mirror your breathing; and the influence you can have on others to make them feel better about you and what you say.

So if you are interested in inspiring others with some winning body language, then read on.

But before we get right into how breathing affects an audience and how to use your breathing patterns to create a positive atmosphere among people at work, it is important first that you understand the details of why we breathe, how we breathe, and what breathing does to our body and our mind.

The Basics of Breathing

Breathing takes oxygen into and carbon dioxide out of the body. Aerobic organisms (that's us) require oxygen to create energy via a process called *respiration*. To put it simply, what happens is that biochemical energy that is locked within the nutrients we eat is converted via oxidization and reduction into the body's "universal energy currency," adenosine triphosphate (ATP), which drives all biological processes. Oxygen molecules are required for the oxidation process involved in ATP production, and the carbon dioxide is taken away from this process as a by-product. All of this can be described by the following simple biochemical equation:

$$\text{Food} + \text{oxygen} = \text{carbon dioxide} + \text{water} + \text{energy}$$

So we breathe in air containing oxygen to convert food into a more universal and usable form of energy to run our body and our mind. We expel carbon dioxide as a by-product of this process.

Active Breathing

Breathing in, or inhaling, is usually an active movement involving the contraction of the diaphragm (the sheet of muscle extending across the bottom of the rib cage), pulling it downward into the belly and increasing the thoracic volume (the space available in the chest cavity). This is known as *negative-pressure breathing*. This process works in conjunction with the intercostal muscles connected to the rib cage. Contraction of these muscles lifts the rib cage, thus aiding the increase in the total thoracic volume. This decreases the pressure inside the lungs and creates a partial vacuum. Air then flows in to fill the vacuum produced in the lungs.

Conversely, exhaling involves the relaxation of the diaphragm, which compresses the lungs, effectively decreasing their thoracic volume while increasing the pressure inside them. The intercostal muscles simultaneously relax, further decreasing the volume of the lungs. This increased pressure forces air out of the lungs. These processes are shown in Figure 4.1.

OK, this may sound crazy-complicated to you, and so you may be thinking, "It's just breathing, and we do it every day without even thinking—it's none of my business," and you may have a point: unconscious breathing is controlled by specialized centers in the brain stem (the reptilian brain) that automatically regulate the rate and depth of breathing depending on the body's needs at any given time.

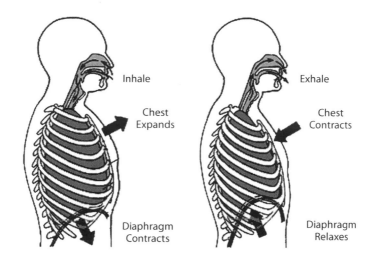

Figure 4.1 Inhaling and Exhaling

Our breathing is controlled by a set of chemical rules and regulations that keep us alive, or, in other words, that stop us from dying (depending on whether your glass of life is half full or half empty). However, there is a certain amount of conscious control that you can have over your breathing. Conscious control of breathing is common in many forms of meditation: for example, in yoga, *pranayama* is all about breath awareness. In sports and physical fitness, breath control is used to regulate such things as oxygen debt in the respiration cycle that can cause a buildup of lactic acid, which in turn causes muscle cramps. In speech and vocal training, breath control is essential for strength and versatility in the voice. No matter what the practice, one learns to discipline one's breathing, consciously at first, but later subconsciously through repetitious enforcement until a habit is formed. So why not use this in business communication?

This conscious control of breath is above and beyond what is needed for "not dying"—it is what is needed to excel at any mental or physical activity. We need it if we are to be energized, engaged, and really fully "alive" in body and mind, and not just "desk jockeying" at the office. The levels of oxygen required for peak performance are way higher than those for a "resting state."

Weird as Folk

I spent a great part of my time at university studying the world of shamanism and its use of movement to open up the psyche. I researched, trained and practiced in the use of masks as utilized by the ancient shamans, and how they and the other members of the tribe would dance to represent the movements of that animal in order to contact and commune with the animal's spirit. In fact, I had been exposed to this from a very early age by performing British folk dance, which is laden with animism and sympathetic magic (the idea that everything has a spirit or essence that can be manipulated via imitative and corresponding symbolic gestures to, in response, control the material world). It became clear to me that the point of this ancient practice was that if you learned through ritual art to move like an animal, you could, through limbic resonance, gain an understanding of the prey's fundamental thought processes and thus gain an advantage when you were hunting or defending yourself against that animal. This pagan art of magic was not hocus-pocus but a competitive advantage. I wondered in how many other fields outside of the arts this ancient knowledge could be played out, and I quickly hit upon business and politics as a huge possibility.

Hyperventilation

If a healthy person were to voluntarily stop breathing (i.e., hold his breath) for a long enough amount of time, he would lose consciousness, and the body would resume breathing on its own, using its unconscious survival mechanism. The results of breathing, consciously or unconsciously, in such a way that only small amounts of oxygen are taken into the bloodstream is known as *hypoventilation*. The opposite of this is *hyperventilation*, which is achieved by shallow, fast breathing. This causes a drop in carbon dioxide to below normal levels, lowering blood acidity (respiratory alkalosis) and confusing the brain into thinking that it has more oxygen than is actually present. This causes the constriction of blood vessels to the brain as a response to the presumed oxygen overabundance, when in fact there is a deficiency. Hyperventilating can cause blood oxygen to go to dangerously low levels. Stress and anxiety and sometimes a full-scale panic attack are common side effects of hyperventilation, with symptoms including weakness; dizziness; tight, tingling, and numb mouth, hands, and feet; blurred vision; racing heartbeat; and faintness, to name just a few.

Some of those symptoms may be all too familiar to any business communicator under stress. When you are under stress, you are likely to hypo- or hyperventilate, and both of these conditions adversely affect the levels of carbon dioxide in your bloodstream, causing energy to be suppressed, diverted, or overdriven in areas of the body or the brain—not a good ecosystem for the growth of inspirational communication between people.

However, in between hypo- and hyperventilation is the right breathing rate and volume that gives the right levels of oxygen and carbon dioxide for the job your body and your mind want to do, a breathing pattern that is ready to adapt to the needs of the body and the mind, allowing you to be "present" to the current environment and alert to future possibilities.

Exercise: Apples and Oranges

So we know that breathing consists of an out breath and an in breath, and right now we are going to discover the effects of each on both the body and the mind of the members of any audience to which you are making a presentation, whether it is a board meeting, a casual chat, or an all-out media circus. Follow these instructions to understand and experience one of the most amazing psychophysical properties of breathing, and to understand how you can use it to persuade and influence nonverbally.

In just one moment, you are going to close your eyes and picture a fruit in your mind. Before you are told which fruit you are to imagine, be aware that the first time you try this, you are going to breathe only *out* as you picture that fruit. No breathing in—just quickly *breathe out*, expel all air, and try to get an image of that fruit in your head. When the breath is over, remember the look and qualities of the fruit that you had in your head. So, breathe out now and imagine an *orange*.

OK, now you are going to do this again with a different fruit and a different way of breathing. This time, you will *breathe in* and imagine the fruit. After imagining this fruit during one single relaxed breath in, you will again remember the qualities of the second imagined fruit. So you are going to breathe in—ready? Breathe in now and imagine an *apple*.

Right—now think about the difference between the apple and the orange (other than the obvious difference that one is an apple and one is an orange). What were the differences in how you imagined, experienced, and appreciated the different fruits? Were there different levels of detail, intensity, and dimensions between the two? Were there different ways in which you sensed each one in your mind's eye and a different feeling from one as opposed to the other? Was it "apples and oranges" in more ways than one?

For your reference, here is what others tend to experience during this experiment.

Out with the Old

The orange that was imagined when breathing out tends to be small in the mind's eye, diminishing or moving away from the viewer; often it is in black and white or a simple monochrome. Many people see the fruit as being shriveled or wrinkled, and some will even see it as rotting. There are also many cases in which viewers see maggots or worms coming out of the fruit—so not to worry if it went that far for you, because you are not at all alone in what imagining on an out breath does for you.

In with the New

In the case of imagining the apple while breathing in, the kind of experience that others have is that the apple is large in the mind's eye and getting bigger. It is often pictured in bright, full color. Some people perceive it as being fresh and can even taste or smell it; in some cases the viewer automatically opens up the apple in her imagination and can see inside it; and for some, without prompt or instruction, the apple can be seen on a tree and as part of a larger orchard.

So we used two fruits—but the qualities of the experience were very different depending on whether you were breathing in or breathing out.

Past the Sell-By Date

The out breath tends to produce an experience that is less vibrant, narrower, and pessimistic. Why? Because the brain is not getting the influx of oxygen that it needs to operate to the fullest capacity. On the out breath, there is no oxygen to spare, and so the brain does not have the energy needed for opening up some higher levels of thinking. Depressed breathing creates a rather depressed attitude greeting everything the brain encounters. Scope is decreased and diminished, because to open out scope will take more brainpower, more oxygen to fuel it, and potentially more energy in the body to deal with the more expansive world that is perceived. If the brain finds that you are breathing out at the point when you want to be imaginative, it just can't let you do this because it fears that the oxygen that is available will be needed for "not dying"—it has a glass-is-half-empty mentality with regard to oxygen levels in the body and the brain. It does not have the excess capacity at this point to really live more expansively!

No surprise, then, that breathing out is often called *expiring*. When you breathe out, you *expire*, and expiry means that it is all over!

Fresh In Today

In stark contrast, when you breathe in, you *inspire*. The ideas that you can get in your mind are fuller, brighter, and more positively biased. Not only this, but when you are breathing in, you have the capacity to investigate inside an idea and also place it in a wider context. Scope is broadened, and more categories are opened. With more oxygen comes more energy and a potential surplus that can be put toward thought and action beyond mere survival.

Now think—what if you could be breathing in an inspirational way all the time when you are speaking? Of course, we all know that you have to breathe out at some point, but if you could breathe in such a way that you expired less, then, strange as it may seem, you would think better, find more opportunities, and have a more positive outlook and internal process. Not only that, but remember that as long as you are giving out clear physical signals, any audience to which you are speaking is predisposed and pro-grammed at a base level to mirror you, or copy your action. If you could send out a clear and continuous physical signal that you are breathing in an inspired way, then every member of your audience would be influenced to copy you, unconsciously. Your listeners would be persuaded to be open, positive, and inspired. They would accept your content and open it out in their own minds to bigger and better prospects.

If the sender of any message is also providing or modeling a physical frame of inspiration (an oxygen and so an energy surplus), then the receivers, who we know will copy that physical frame (and create an oxygen and energy surplus within themselves) are very likely to fall into a mental state of inspiration. This will force the receivers to view and translate the content as fitting into that category, because, as we have already seen, we agree with what we see and believe what we feel. And ultimately, that is the influencing factor as to why people say, "I felt inspired by that speech!" "Our meeting was inspirational," or "Your leadership inspired me to act."

On the flip side, when the speaker gets a bored response from her audience, it is probably not because her content is intrinsically boring. It is more likely that her breathing is expired, causing the audience to "die" of boredom. By breathing in such a way that you are depleting your own body and mind of the energy-producing oxygen, you will also cause the same thing to happen to your audience as well. When you close down your own body and mind, the audience will copy your leadership and do the same.

Now, the good news. There is a physical state that causes both you and your audience to go into a state of inspiration, and it is called being *on the in breath*. Performers have used this technique for thousands of years to be sure that they have enough oxygen to maintain their energy and therefore their *presence*. As Brian Bates, the former chair of psychology at Sussex University and Royal Academy of Dramatic Art acting trainer, states in his chapter on charisma from *Way of the Actor*, "Oxygen becomes a psychological force and soon is converted by the mind of the actor into a physical force. . . . We want that power in the stage presence of the actor." Theatrical master and anthropologist Eugenio Barba states in *The Secret Art of the Performer* that the term *bayu*, meaning breath, is used in ancient Balinese theater to denote the

A Valuable Tool

It did not take long for me to formulate a theory that all effective communication is designed to either move us toward our goals or move us away from threats to accomplishing those goals. Anything else is "spam" (abuse of the communication system), which is bad, or "play" (communication for the sheer pleasure of it), which is fine. However, the majority of business communication that I came across at every level too often seemed to me to be designed (by accident or plain ignorance) to cause a standstill—a freeze response in which just nothing happens. So I thought, "If I can help people become aware of communication that is capable of moving themselves and others toward both personal and organizational goals, then that would improve their performance during critical times and give them a massive competitive advantage." Others in the communication training world seemed to be concentrating on "more and better formed content" or psychological coaching around intention as the universal remedy, and I could already see that before the content could ever be assimilated by an audience, and intentions met, a human, emotional connection needed to be made so that the audience would trust and accept the message. My major understanding was of the tool for connecting humans known as nonverbal communication, which it turns out is the major tool that all of us use all the time, but unconsciously. If this was my hammer, then I would make every problem look like a nail and find the nonverbal and structural solution to the business communication problems presented to me.

increase in power that "elevates" the body and generates a feeling of "life" in any act. A performer's breathing alone can fill an audience with a sense of expectation and energy for the the actions he is selling for the story he is telling. These states are not achieved via such common respiratory techniques as "breathing from the belly," so often presented by business presentation trainers as a cure-all. If you want the real secret of how to breathe in a way that inspires the audience to listen, then here's how you do it.

On the In Breath

Stand up right now (or stay sitting if standing up is impractical at the moment). Begin expanding yourself upward—gently cause your body to straighten up. Pretend that you are being pulled up by a string that comes from the very crown of your head. Do not let your heels leave the ground. As you allow yourself to be pulled up from the crown of your head, lengthening along your spine, make sure that you remain well connected to the ground. Some people describe a feeling of lightness in the body while they are performing this exercise, but you are not trying to act like a floating apparition here. Remain pulled up and fully connected with the floor. Now check how your breathing is.

Can you feel yourself still breathing in and out, inspiring and expiring? Do you notice, however, that when you breathe in this position, you are predominantly on the in breath? Still breathing in and out, yet "suspended" within a physical feeling of more in breath than out breath. Your breathing is not rushed, and it is not shallow; you are taking in plenty of air (and so oxygen), but without hyperventilating. You will already be starting to feel very positive on this new in-breath pattern. You may have noticed that you have a gentle, open smile that comes with this physical state. This is, of course, great news, because such a smile is inviting to the members of your audience, and they will mirror it back to you. What's more, this is a simple by-product of being on the in breath.

You may also notice, after breathing this way for a while, that your perceptions are opening up: you may be experiencing a widening of your peripheral vision or more color, brightness, and detail in what you see. Have you noticed more acuity in your hearing? With more oxygen, the brain can afford to deal with (process) more information—it is happy for you to see and hear more. This is great for you as an influencer: the more information you have, the more power you have to persuade.

Notice that it takes energy to sustain this elongated spine and light feeling in the body and still be grounded; but happily you have more energy because of the type of breathing that you are experiencing. I sometimes refer to this suspended, light, energetic, soft yet springy feeling as being in an "available" state.

On the Out Breath

Now let's try the opposite. Allow your spine to sink, and let your stomach cave in. Cast off the feeling of lightness and the feeling of a pull toward the sky. Exchange this for a pull toward the ground. Have you already noticed your breathing pattern changing and the more depressing thoughts that go with it?

Notice the difference in your face. Where is the open, gentle smile now that your eyes are gazing down at the floor instead of at the horizon? You will notice with this that many of the colors and sounds in the world have disappeared. The world seems less available to you and you no doubt feel less available in turn to the world.

Now quickly put your body back into the position for being on the in breath. How quickly do you feel more inspired? That's how quickly an audience can follow you from one state to another. That is how quickly you can either depress or inspire the person or crowd that you are communicating with. Figure 4.2 shows the difference in physical position for the two kinds of breaths.

A Rousing Speech

Note that this is all done with your *body*—not the body of your *text*. The words of a presentation, speech, or conversation are the icing on the cake or the sauce on the pasta. Get the base right, and what you add to give it intellectual weight can be minimal but have maximum effect. If you build a strong foundation with the techniques discussed so far in this book, you will find that your content has more effect on the audience by going

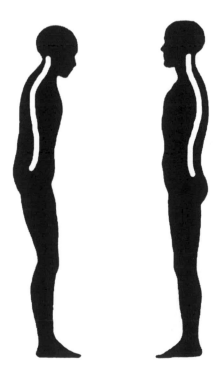

Figure 4.2 The Physicality of the Out Breath versus the In Breath

deeper into their minds in a more positive way. No longer will you have to feel that you must "pad out" your content like a schoolroom essay (just trying to get marks for length of content) because the structure, which in this case is your body, will give your audience a feeling of trust and inspiration, and your content will ride the wave of this positive perception. It is not the speech but the speaker that wins trust and inspires action. Audiences focus first on the messages that they get from watching the bulk of the speaker's body mass. People tend to judge someone's general intention from the way that person carries herself, and they can register her emotion from the expression on her face. The body language reader quickly begins to mirror that body physically, including monitoring the movement of the chest to mirror breathing patterns and become synchronized with the levels of oxygen in others' bloodstreams to gain a resonance with the attitude.

Breathe and the World Breathes with You

Here's something more, just in case you need convincing further.

You will now start to notice how, over the centuries, what the really great artists—the people who make us laugh and cry and wonder; the people who fill our world with color and dark stories that can fill us with fear and provoke us to action; the people who fill the world with music that moves us— have actually been doing is creating *strong, clear rhythms* that our breathing can join in on. They are geniuses at provoking us to breathe in patterns that strongly influence our feelings, and so our perception of the world, going back to the very first shamanic performers.

For example, watch a great film, but *turn off the sound*. Can you instantly see how you start to breathe along with the actors? That is the film's route to your feelings, by having good actors who communicate in a way that allows the audience to *join in on the feeling*. The actors are no longer actually having the feelings they created for you and captured on film—but you are! They are not creating the emotion right now—you are doing it for them! Their work is inspirational: they breathe, you copy, and the legacy is that which you feel.

Notice that as the film cuts from shot to shot, you are also breathing along with *that* rhythm—and this is creating tension and feeling in your body. That is the artistry of the film editor. He influences and persuades you with the rhythm of the cut, provoking you to think and feel with the film and the stars acting in it in a certain manner and with definite feelings often pre-planned by the film's director. As the radical psychiatrist, expert on the mass psychology of fascism and early architect of Gestalt therapy—which concentrates on the therapeutic experience of the present, Wilhelm Reich recognized and stated "Emotional and physical states can be altered by changing the breathing pattern."

To experience this further, now turn up the sound and see how the music, the *score* of the film, with its own rhythm, *conspires* (as the word suggests, *con*, meaning "with," and *spire*, meaning "breath") with all the other artistry in the film. The music binds together the rhythm of the actors and the rhythm of the picture with sound so that there is no doubt as to the feelings that are being promoted to the audience. You conspire along with it all as well, as you respond by having similar feelings within you. The film is not the feeling—it is simply the instruction manual for how you get to it. It is the map to the feeling. It is not the message; the message happens in you. Great filmmaking is nonverbal influence and persuasion at some of its very best.

Inspire and Motivate

So, now you are beginning to see how you yourself can influence those around you with a simple breathing technique that paves the way for your audience to think and feel positively toward you and receptive to your verbal ideas and instructions. Being on the in breath causes your audience to be more available to you. You now simply need to start breathing predominantly on the in breath every time you want to inspire others. They will copy your body language and will be truly inspired in themselves. It only remains for you to move that inspiration through to real action: to get those around you motivated and actually putting your ideas into physical form.

Now, how can you use body language to influence others and persuade them to act—to literally motivate (move) them into a state of acting out your message? Of course there is a way.

Chapter 4 Quick Study

In Breath: There are two ways of breathing: in and out. When you are predominantly on more of an in breath than an out breath, you supply more oxygen to your body and your brain. You have more oxygen resources for physical and mental opportunities. Your listeners mirror this style of breathing and, in turn, become more open and available to the opportunities that you as a communicator can offer them. They can conspire with you to be inspired.

Just Do This Now

1. Be on the in breath when you communicate.

2. Use the in breath to engage your audience with expectation.

3. Use the out breath to deflate or disappoint your audience and maybe create an atmosphere of negativity or depression around certain aspects of a communication when this may be to your and their advantage.

Chapter 4 Case Study

Theory to Practice: Lightening the Load

Fresh off a strategic selling workshop, Kevin clarifies to himself his desire to introduce new service options to the portfolio of one of his "high-opportunity" clients. He has winning rapport with his key decision maker, Alice, and understands her hot buttons. In the discussion, he is able to expose the gap in the current agreement and create a good degree of fear and uncertainty. To his surprise, Alice fails to get excited when he presents his "solution." She seems defeated by his line of questioning. The meeting ends with both of them depressed: she because she sees the problems; he because there is no deal yet.

Insight

Change is risky, and people are risk-averse. Fear of consequences can counter the inertia and encourage action rather than complacency. This logic is sound, although an interesting paradox is that fear brings negative (out-breath) emotions, but new thought requires positive (in-breath) thinking.

To use this technique, Kevin would pause and take an exaggerated in breath right before moving into his description of a potential solution. Interestingly, this may be difficult to overdo because taking a deep breath is a reasonable human action and not too big for the business world. This simple action, if timed correctly, can move the client into a more positive and receptive state.

Provocation

Have you found some of concepts or practices in this book difficult to take in and assimilate? New ideas are often difficult to accept. Why not take the advice I gave in the preface of this book and "take a breath" before reading on. That in breath is designed to help you be available to these ideas and move forward positively. Try it.

Injecting Excitement into Your Gestures

Are You Feeling It?

Without passion you don't have energy; without energy you have nothing.

—Donald Trump

In this chapter you'll learn:

- How to get some passion back into your business life
- Movement that motivates yourself and others
- Speaking from the heart rather than from the hip
- Nonverbal melodramatics for alpha males
- How to raise the heart rate in the board-room

Why is there no passion in the workplace? So many business theorists extol the virtues of going about the workday with a sense of high energy, vitality, and a fire in your heart for the work that you do. And great business minds, for example, investor Warren Buffett, ranked by *Forbes* in 2008 as the richest person in the world, says of the ideal colleague or employee: "I look for a person with passion for the job, good communicators."

It's easy for a lot of people to get passionate about their sports team; it's easier for even more people to get passionate about music; and it's tough for a marriage to survive if one is not passionate about one's partner. Some folks are even passionate about the food and drink that they consume every day. Yet most of us ultimately spend most of our time in life at work, and for much of that time you may be *passionless*.

If you want to be persuasive and influential, then passion is going to be one of the great keys to getting everyone on board, motivated, and actively seeing to the work that you need them to do to help build your inspirational vision. You will need to be able to enroll others in your winning vision by displaying inspired, trustworthy, and passionate business body language.

From the techniques we have already detailed, you have the *TruthPlane* for trust, and you have the *in breath* for inspiration. Right now, we need to deal with *passion* by introducing you to the *PassionPlane*, a horizontal plane of gesture that raises you to a motivational level every time you speak to an audience by bringing out the fire in other people's hearts. You see, you may be trustworthy and so trusted, and you may be inspired and inspirational, but as yet that does not mean that anyone will actually do anything for you. You need to be passionate about what you're communicating if you want to be able to motivate others into action.

This idea explains why, in a workplace, on a project, or during a sales call, you can be "on message" yet get no result: because the message itself is not enough to create action—to get us moving. We must be motivated toward a desire. Build desire and you can create a compelling feeling of enthusiasm for action. And for those of you who have ever desired anything in your life (not wanted or needed, but *desired*), you will understand that this is a feeling and not an intellectual state. And this desire is created in the audience by the passion expressed by you, the speaker.

So first of all, let's look at this feeling of passion and find out exactly what it is, understand how and why it exists, and uncover what it looks like so that we can reproduce it ourselves. We need to examine passion so that we can understand the advantages and disadvantages of summoning it up and learn how to control it in ourselves, using it most effectively to invite others to share in our excitement and to motivate and move them into action in the most professional manner.

A Brief History of High Emotions

The word *passion* is most probably derived from the Latin *pati*, meaning "to suffer" (as seen, for example, in the Christian church, where the recounting of Jesus' crucifixion is known as "the Passion"). The common modern understanding of the word is that it denotes intense feeling and can be applied to any kind of feeling. You can be passionate in all kinds of ways: passionately angry or passionately in love—indeed, you can be passionate and intense about any feeling known to humankind, and there are many, many feelings. Let's look at some to understand passion more fully.

Take the example of love, which we could say embraces the more complex, subtle, and extreme emotions of affection and maybe even lust. And within affection, you may have experienced and seen in others the more complicated and subtle states such as adoration, fondness, attraction, tenderness, or compassion. So one feeling often has many more facets or subfeelings to it.

There is an abundance of feelings, and many psychological and social theorists over the years have come up with their own lists of these feelings and what they look like. However, there is one list that should stand out for any student of universal body language: the list proposed by Dr. Paul Ekman, a psychologist who has been a pioneer in the study of emotions and their relation to facial expressions since 1954. He is considered one of the 100 most eminent psychologists of the twentieth century.

Universal Feelings

From his research across the globe, Ekman found that many emotional facial expressions are not culturally determined, but are universal and thus biological in origin. The facial expressions that he originally found to be the same universally includes those displaying anger, disgust, fear, joy, sadness, and surprise. There's more to come about Dr. Ekman and his importance to the world of body language, but for now it is enough to note that all of these feelings expressed through facial manipulations can be intense and passionate, and, as Ekman has found, they can be communicated universally. The important thing for our purposes in business is to understand how to share our feelings appropriately with an audience, giving our listeners enough intensity of feeling that they feel compelled to join in and go with our passion—in other words, we must make our passion their passion, and cause them to be motivated enough by it to act.

Let's look at this problem from a biological point of view and see how the body can be used as a solution.

Bio-Solutions

Place your hands in the TruthPlane and monitor your approximate breathing rate and the extent to which you are filling your lungs with air. You will probably notice that when you have your hands in the TruthPlane, you are breathing steadily and fairly deeply—right down into your diaphragm.

Now shift your hands up to your chest height and notice the difference. What has happened to your breathing rate now? Into which part of your lungs are you now predominantly bringing oxygen? You will have noticed that when you set your hands in the chest area, and specifically the horizontal plane of gesture that comes out from just a couple of inches above the sternum (the center and bottom of the rib cage, at exactly the level at which you can best feel your heartbeat), your breathing rate quickly increases and you breathe more into your chest than into your belly. Some of you may have already noticed an increase in your heart or pulse rate that automatically goes along with this.

It seems that gesturing with your hands at chest level automatically increases your breathing rate and heart rate and produces a slightly shallower style of breathing. And you will also notice that it quickly creates way more energy and more than an edge of excitement in you.

Now drop your hands down by your sides and notice what happens as you drop into the GrotesquePlane and naturally onto the *out breath* and into an *expired* physical posture. What happened to the energy you had— your feeling, your sense of motivation, and your thought process in general? You will be feeling the effects of a more depressed breathing right now. As you are in this position, imagine giving a speech or a presentation, or even having a conversation, and start to speak the words that you would be using. Can you quickly hear the predominantly downward intonation in your voice, denoting depression, negativity, or ending, when you are in the GrotesquePlane? Now let's compare this to passion.

Speaking from the Heart

Look even further into how this horizontal level of gesture changes the voice: once again shift your hands up to your chest level and carry on with giving the speech or presentation or having a conversation. What do you notice immediately? Listen to how the pitch of your voice has risen considerably. Also notice the increased upward inflection of the voice, which implies nonverbally that there is still more to come: it creates tension and suspense, causing an audience to be hooked into the sound in order to hear it be completed with a downward ("it's over") tonality. By using this intonation, you are instigating the members of your audience to demand completion of the musical cadence, and they will be hooked until they are satisfied. Do you also notice that your body feels more suspended? There may be a feeling of "something is about to happen" when you have your hands up gesturing in the chest area. The mirroring or copying that you by now know to expect from your listeners causes their breathing to also be suspended. They are now looking for a deep out breath and will remain hooked by you until you let them off the hook by giving a strong out breath into an instruction for action. And with all the energy this state has built up in them, there is a surplus of energy they need to expend with action (or risk a build-up of toxins). Your call for action is all the excuse the body needs to redress their energetic balance by getting up a going for it.

The excitement from the energy you are creating, both in your body and in the tone of your voice, is bestowed upon the verbal content of your speech. When your hands come up to your chest and you gesture and speak, there is an energetic buzz, particularly in comparison to the loss of energy and potential depression in the GrotesquePlane and the level-headed stability of the TruthPlane. Gesturing from the chest area literally raises your oxygen level and so your energy level, gets your blood pumping from your heart, and compels those around you to do and feel the same. This is why I call this area the PassionPlane (see Figure 5.1).

Figure 5.1 Mirroring in the PassionPlane

The Biomechanics of Passion

Why does this technique work so well to raise the energy and ignite the passion within you and within those who make up your audience, embedding in even the most supposedly boring subject matter qualities of excitement and extreme interest? First, you are gesturing in a very safe area of your body. After all, while the chest, like the belly, contains vital organs, it is covered by the hard bones of the rib cage. This arrangement gives us a relatively high level of safety in this area, maybe even a feeling of invulnerability. You can afford to be more expansive and step up your energy from this area because you are less afraid of being damaged there.

Certainly we see that in aggressive posturing between human beings, the chest is displayed and the arms are opened out in this area, perhaps drawing any aggressor's attention away from our very vulnerable middle area and toward this very safe area, where less damage can be easily inflicted. Notice how in fighting sports such as boxing, an attack is traditionally made not at the chest area, but rather at the belly, head, neck, lower back, and limbs. You may see aggressive pushing at the chest area, or warning people back at this height, but again, this is relatively safe compared to attracting an attack on the soft and delicate stomach area.

Fighting For Breath

When I studied the movement and behavior of animals many years ago, I gained a great deal of knowledge about aggressive and passive body language. It soon became clear that the martial arts provided a fount of very old and powerful psychophysical knowledge around this area. I studied one-on-one with a master of martial arts (in return for some acting training) in order to understand more about the balance of the body and how it coped with stress or could be destabilized by placing specific twists along the spine that not only unbalanced physically but also mentally and psychologically. (This lasted until I was accidentally knocked out—ouch!) The learning that had the most impact (apart from now being sure to duck when a foot comes toward your head at 40 mph and 1,000 pounds of pressure) was the exact way in which breath affected both visualization and action. We would spend time breaking dense wooden boards, during which I would deliberately reverse the usual breathing for this (visualize the board breaking on an out breath and strike it on an in breath), often, as you might imagine, crying out with the pain that the board inflicted on me. But when I applied the correct breathing—visualizing the board parting in two on the in breath and just made a relaxed, soft strike on a clear out breath, my hand sliced through the thick wood like a hot knife through butter. There was nothing mysterious—just simple psychophysiology. Basic physics, biology, and artistry wrapped into one. My other great learnings were centered on the fact that one of the fundamental ways of dealing with aggression is simply not to be near it in the first place.

The Passion of the Chest

The chest has an element of bravado about it. Think about any of the great film action heroes and how large their chest is as they square up to the enemy. Think about the chest-beating ape that shows dominance over other males and his territory by displaying his upper body strength. Therefore, gestures in the PassionPlane can also easily be perceived as aggressive. The energy created by working within this GesturePlane can become very high, and if it is not controlled skillfully, it can make the communicator come across as too forward. Indeed, if a communicator raises her energy level too much, appears to be all over the place, and gestures frenetically and in an overly aggressive manner in the PassionPlane, she can be seen as pointlessly melodramatic in a way that is just not possible in say the TruthPlane. Indeed, if one's gestures in the chest area are wild, the energy can become so high and unrestrained that the mouth begins to work faster than the brain, and words become garbled and nonsensical. At that point, the communicator looks not just completely out of control, but in some cases utterly crazy.

High adrenaline combined with high passion can be a difficult combination for the business communicator to handle. In the heat of the moment, with adrenalin on overload, the presenter quickly starts to breathe very high in the chest, with short, sharp breaths. These breaths can easily produce a perfect physical environment for hyperventilation and the faint and tingly feelings that come with it, or even a sense of panic. If you lose control of your energy in the PassionPlane, you also stand a good chance of moving into a state of heightened aggression (especially if you have no way out of the situation), which is mirrored, in turn, by your receivers (audience, coworkers, and so on), and the next thing you know, the whole room is unconsciously having a secondhand panic attack. This is perhaps the worst possible outcome for a shareholders' meeting.

This is why you must tread quite carefully with the motivating and energizing factors in this particular plane of gesture, using the TruthPlane alongside it to bring balance to the passion. Be very particular about when you use the PassionPlane and when you use the TruthPlane. In general, you should use the PassionPlane to frame content that you wish to come across as exciting, energetic, or even aggressive, and use the TruthPlane for content that you wish to come across as factual, honest, and sincerely felt. For example, in the CFO's "It's been a great year" speech, when it is delivered using the PassionPlane, it could be highly motivating and inspire the audience to buy more stock—but do we feel from the delivery that we can really *trust* the information? It could easily look like a dramatic exaggeration, and that is a potential problem with the PassionPlane. Maybe the results should be delivered in the TruthPlane and the future expectations be delivered in the PassionPlane; then the audience can both be assured that the stock is healthy now *and* be engaged in the company's future prosperity through the speaker's passion. On this point, also remember that any feeling you talk about from the PassionPlane will be pushed into a more intense delivery of that emotion. Just for fun, try the exercise below.

The "I Love You" Exercise

All you are going to be saying in this exercise is the phrase, "I love you." Now put your hands down by your sides in the GrotesquePlane and try saying the words. How does it feel? Would you believe it if you heard somebody else tell you that in the same intonation that you just used? Now put your hands at navel height, the TruthPlane, and say the words. How did that feel to you? Now put your hands at chest height, the PassionPlane, and say the words one last time.

Did you notice the subtle yet profound differences among the three? The words remained the same each time, but there is a clear difference in the intention and meaning of the message when you change the position of your hands. Which version you did you believe most? Which was most sincere, which seemed the most excited, and which was the most disengaged? The answer should be immediately obvious.

Artistic Temperament

This PassionPlane enjoys a long tradition of hosting feelings at extreme levels. Master artists across the globe have known for centuries that depicting figures that are gesturing from the chest will give an audience an instant feeling of high energy, high emotion, and active motivation.

Take for example the quite common Christian icon of Christ on a wooden cross portrayed with his arms in the PassionPlane, representing an image of passionate love for humankind. A good example of which is the one looking over the city of Rio de Janeiro, Brazil (Figure 5.2), where the cross is not shown, but the figure remains in the PassionPlane—an inspirational and motivating image of passion for many in that city and across the world.

Now, it so happens that much of the military and judicial history suggests that a Roman crucifixion was more likely performed with hands far above the head, putting the figure into more of a Y shape or even elongated into an I shape rather than the traditional cross quite common in Christian images.

Figure 5.2 Passion O Cristo Redentor

But artists know that when they place the figure in the general posture of a more historically accurate Roman crucifixion, with the hands way above the head, the image is more tragic or depressing: one of surrender.

Whether you are in the business of evangelism or out there evangelizing about your business, people need to see, hear, and feel the passion behind your message in order to be motivated and join in. Remember, though, that if you are overly passionate, you may be viewed as out of control and overemotional. Generally, emotion is considered relatively dangerous, as it is very unpredictable. We don't like to be around someone when his emotions seem to be out of control. However, we are fascinated and engaged by emotions when they are under control. That is why we are more able to watch extreme violence from the safe distance of a film screen but would without doubt run a mile were it for real. It is the same for business: the controlled passion of a CEO for her team—say, a great speech that talks about their brilliant work with great fervor, but from the distance of a stage presentation—may be more palatable than the CEO's leaping into the audience and hugging and kissing everyone. Both can be equally passionate, yet one might feel more appropriate because it is whole lot safer. Test out this GesturePlane for yourself, and learn how to create a controlled sense and feeling of passion around anything you say and so afford your audience the extra energy this provides to be motivated to join you. In later chapters, I will explain how to mix this PassionPlane with other Gesture-Planes to create balance and narrative flow in your nonverbal influence.

Passion is important to business and in the business messages that you send out. A passionate, energized body has the potential psychological effect of influencing an audience's perception in quite positive ways: not least that your listeners will feel and mirror your excitement. Next, you will learn how to support what you've learned so far by creating positive impressions with your facial expressions also, helping your audience to understand that you are open and here to help.

Chapter 5 Quick Study

Passion is fundamental to motivating the members of your audience to action by helping them to understand your energy and giving them energetic movements to mirror and a surplus of energy that needs expending—predisposing them to execute the actions you ask for.

Just Do This Now

1. Gesture with your hands in the PassionPlane—at chest level—to bring passion to your communication and raise the heart rate and activity of both you and your audience.

2. Bring product samples or reports up into the chest area to give them an air of excitement. Take them to the TruthPlane to give them trusted status or drop them into the GrotesquePlane to demote them.

3. The PassionPlane can create a more aggressive and argumentative atmosphere. Push yourself and others into gesturing in the chest area to create a more passionate environment for discord—if this is what you are looking for!

Chapter 5 Case Study

Theory to Practice—Letting Off Steam

"Why did I have to book this one in the FishBowl meeting room?" Stacey asks herself, as the client does not even sit down before launching into an uninformed rant about the preliminary results of the latest online ad campaign. The FishBowl is pretty much soundproof, but it is the only meeting room in the agency without opaque glass. Now the whole office is getting a crystal-clear picture of her angry and upset client yet can't hear the unreasonable nonsense that is going with it and would mitigate the negative way the image alone reflects on Stacey and her work. She could mistakenly lose office status fast if she does not do the right thing.

As the account team leader, Stacey chooses to sit down and visibly sustains an open gesture in the TruthPlane while the client's outburst quickly calms. By the end of the meeting, the conversation has become quite productive.

Insight

Given this scenario, Stacey probably did the right thing. Staying physically lower than the other person, especially if you expose your middle (e.g., by pushing your chair away from the table a bit), will reduce the intensity of such an "attack." It will also shorten the length of time the attack continues, thereby making it less conspicuous, which is obviously a concern for Stacey.

Provocation

Do you like to win? Can you imagine yourself ever losing first in order to win later on?

Faces Tell the Whole Story

Using Your Head for a Change

Other men are lenses through which we read our own minds.
—Ralph Waldo Emerson

In this chapter you'll learn:

- The secrets of physical mind control
- How we mistake tired leaders for liars
- More motivating gestures
- Facial coding for compelling communication
- Why Botox can kill your message

B usiness deals would be much easier to negotiate if we were able to read other people's minds and understand what they really want or need. With that kind of knowledge, we would undoubtedly be able to influence the other party to see our point of view every time (or at least understand what she really thought of us!). Unfortunately, most of us cannot read other people's minds. Or can we?

Well, technically we can't read minds. What we can do, however, is read other people's faces, and in many cases that can turn out to be the same thing. We often hear that the eyes are the windows to the soul, and some scientists have found that they can tell character types from a microscopic study of the iris. Dr. Mats Larsson has led research at the Center for Developmental Research, Örebro University, that confirms that a gene called Pax6 is involved in both the development of the eye and the development of an area of the brain involved in conflict detection and emotional awareness. Larsson found that the presence of "crypts" (pits found in the iris) were significantly associated with the personality characteristics of warmth and trust, whereas "contraction furrows" were associated with impulsiveness.

On a larger scale, certainly every muscle movement that a person makes with his face potentially affects what others think about him. Facial cues are hugely important when you are up close and personal in business, as in life in general. However, it is very difficult to read another person's body language 100 percent correctly. For example, is the person with her arms crossed being willfully nonreceptive, fending off the cold, or simply trying to stay awake and engaged? It's impossible to know this for sure from just that one signal.

So, the business communicator who is skilled in using body language needs to also deliver gestures from in and around the face to most fully ensure the reactions and actions desired from his audience in any given situation. In this chapter, you will learn how to get gestures across with your face and the space around your head so that you can have an even stronger positive influence over the opinions of others and help change their minds, often for the better.

Five Thousand Reasons Why Not

Visual artists for centuries have expressed the beauty and mystery of the human face by capturing the emotions displayed within it in still pictures; scientists, however, are continually discovering that much of the power of the face is encapsulated in the split-second expressions that unconsciously slip across it thousands of times each day—in the "microexpressions" or "microgestures" made popular by the work of Dr. Paul Ekman (and the TV character based on him, Dr. Cal Lightman in the network series *Lie to Me*). These fleeting facial gestures are created with as many as, if not more than, 52 facial muscles (depending on how you categorize them) and the nerves and blood vessels serving them, all built upon the foundation of bone and cartilage and covered by the skin; these facial components can take on as many as 5,000 expressions, from the most obvious grimace to the most subtle eyebrow lift. These play a large part in guiding our lives in terms of how we relate to one another as individuals and the way we connect together as a society every time we meet face to face.

Indeed, the ability to make faces, and to read them, is vital to both our personal interactions with any group or society and the survival of our species as a whole. This is so much the case that the father of the natural selection hypothesis of evolution, Darwin, wrote extensive theories on universal facial expressions, published in his book *The Expressions of the Emotions in Man and Animals* in 1898, and academics such as Ekman have further built upon these ideas that the primary emotions conveyed by the face are universal.

Psychologists too have been studying the human face and scrutinizing its potential hidden code for decades. The face is the most extraordinary communicator, capable of signaling emotion accurately in the blink of an eye, but capable of concealing emotion equally well. As Ekman states in his 1997 book *What the Face Reveals*, "The face is equipped to lie the most and leak the most, and thus can be a very confusing source of information."

Mixed Messages

It would seem that although humans are an intensely social species, and as such are reliant on communication, we are also designed to give mixed messages: combinations of gestures that conceal (or secretly reveal) our intention, our motivation, and the inner workings of our minds. This duplicity is in our very nature.

Before we look at the human face in detail to discover what nonverbal messages we send with any sense of accuracy and assurance about their meaning, let's look at the head area in general and find out what can be done with this physical space in order to communicate our messages nonverbally.

Head Space

You will remember that as human beings, we get a great deal of our information about the world through what we see. We are able to detect patterns through our sight and instantly make judgments based on past experience, or to use instinctual behavior to determine the appropriate action or reaction for us. However, when we listen, the information travels to and is processed by our brain at a much slower rate.

Because of the relative complexity of sound compared to vision, we rely on supplementing the understanding that we receive from sound with the pictures that go with it. Indeed, it has been speculated that because speech-associated gestures could possibly reduce lexical or sentential ambiguity, comprehension should improve in the presence of such gestures. And work by the department of psychology at the University of Chicago has shown that when spoken language is accompanied by meaningful speech-associated gestures, comprehension is improved. Furthermore, when spoken language is accompanied by no gestures at all or gestures that are irrelevant to the verbal material, it takes longer to comprehend speech. In short, it is neurologically simpler for us to understand speech when we see it. But it is not just arm gestures that we are talking about here.

When we listen to someone speak, we are reading that person's lips more than we would ever expect, and looking out for facial and physical gestures that help us to deduce the potential meaning of what is being said exactly. Take this encounter, for example: a colleague approaches you and says, "Have you read the report?" Now, how do you know if this is a question or not? Your colleague does not approach you with a question mark signal (?) on her forehead—or maybe she does. You might see some expression in her face that suggests to you that this is a question—a furrowed brow, for example. However, this furrowed brow could also be interpreted as stress in the communicator: is she asking you whether you have read the report, or is she telling you that you should have read it, and she is angry because she thinks you have not? Maybe you can listen for an upward inflection in the voice, which would suggest that she is asking a question.

You can see that even before you begin to wonder if you heard the words right (because maybe she actually said, "You ready to report?" and waved the meeting agenda at you!), you are looking for some visual signs of meaning and fitting the content to that frame. Next you will look at how the person's lips are moving in order to help you understand the exact words that are being used and correlate this with the supposed meaning, getting a message that is congruent. If the message is incongruent, then you will tend to go with what you see and make what you heard sound like that—and if you can't manage that, then on the whole you will be confused. And so here is the first lesson about head space for the business communicator:

We need to see your face to know more of what you are saying!

Read My Lips

To test just how much your audience relies on seeing your lips move to understand verbal language, try this out on a colleague: go and have a chat and find ways to keep your hands over your mouth throughout. Notice how many misunderstandings occur and how frustrated your colleague gets because he cannot get the message—because he cannot *see* the message. Now bring your hands down to the TruthPlane and see the relief in your colleague's face and body. He can now read your lips and see your intention in your face (as well as being assured by your gestures from the part of your body that engenders the most trust). You may think that even the most naive business communicator would not cover his face when he was speaking; however, you will notice, especially in long meetings at tables, that when the head gets tired (it weighs about 8 to 12 pounds, and the neck can get tired of carrying it), even a seasoned communicator's hands can easily creep up to the chin and the mouth to cup the head with elbows supported on the table to take stress off the neck—something that is comfortable for the person who is holding her head up, but very uncomfortable for the people who are trying to understand and communicate with her because they cannot see her words!

Pants on Fire

The mouth and jaw area of the head I call the horizontal gesture plane of *disclosure*. If the audience members cannot see this area, then they feel as if they are being closed off, and therefore lack information. They can easily turn this feeling into the idea that the communicator is purposely withholding data, or, to put it bluntly, *lying*! Of course, it is not necessarily true that the sender of a message with his hands in this area is lying (to work that out would take far more evidence), but that is often the *feeling* we get when someone speaks to us with his hands in this horizontal plane.

The lesson here is: keep your hands away from your mouth so that everyone can hear your meaning correctly. Conversely, you can use your hands up around your jaw and at mouth level to *funnel* the audience's vision toward your mouth and direct it to your speech—this would be a gesture of disclosure, seen as, "I am telling you everything." Try out this gesture for yourself: bring your hands up to your mouth level and use them to funnel an imagined audience into seeing the mouth area. Can you recognize how it quickly begins to feel as though you are imploring the audience to understand or believe you? You can also probably feel how quickly your energy (physical and mental) rises and becomes quite excited and frantic. Can you feel how your words might run away with you?

On the whole, gesturing around the lower face is to be avoided unless you wish to create a potential feeling of mistrust of the message. For example, try saying this with your hands in the DisclosurePlane: "I have given the board all the information we have on this matter." Remember that we believe what we see, and so if you are covering the message, we are not as able to believe it. So now try the same sentence with your hands in the TruthPlane. You will instantly understand both the merits and the disadvantages of the DisclosurePlane from this exercise, and get a feeling for how using it, especially unknowingly, can create intense distrust in your audience.

Word to the Action

I have studied and performed in many different styles and forms of theater and performance from around the globe. In all of the styles and traditions that I have experienced firsthand, gesture always comes very slightly before the text, not only in performance, but in life. Indeed, there are methods used by directors in rehearsal whereby the movement or choreography of the work is fully organized and worked out *before* adding the text, in order to get the fundamental psychology of the action set to the desires and intentions of the dramatic characters. One exception to gesture coming before text is in comedy—it is easy to get a laugh from an audience by simply putting the text before the action. The incongruity can be anything from subtly humorous to "fall-off-your-chair funny." It is interesting, researching further into this area, to learn that movement is the precursor to language and the thought behind language (brain research now tells us that the nonverbal reactions to our feelings happen well before we can verbalize them). Therefore, it is no surprise that complex rehearsed movement from public speakers can often appear insincere and sometimes plain stupid—not because it is not possible for rehearsed movement and speech to be emotionally authentic (good actors can "fake" that level of sincerity take after take, show after show if they need to), but because for these business presenters, it is quite tricky to connect overly complex and often meaningless movements with text that is complex and all too often lacking intention. The speaker in this context is often content-obsessed; she reads or remembers the words and performs or remembers the movement a second later—too late! That is why I stay well away from choreographing detailed movements with clients. Instead, we work on keeping a simple consistency to their physical movement that will produce big pictures to which their audiences' minds can respond. The speaker, once she is comfortable working within a simple physical framework, is now liberated to allow her own sincere, detailed movement to come out as natural or "authentic" responses to the impulses of the event. She is living in the "here and now" instead of the "back then and rehearsed" mentally uncluttered from having to sustain complex psychological intentions, and gestures, pre-arranged thoughts and rehearsed words. Preparation of the physical vocabulary and availability to the moment is the road to success, not mental or physical rehearsal.

The ThoughtPlane

As the hands move further up the head, they become level with the eyes and the temples. Let's understand the effect that this has on you and anyone with whom you are communicating.

Bring your hands up to your temples, put your fingers on the temple area, and try delivering this sentence again: "I have given the board all the information we have on this matter." Can you feel the mental strain that this gesture gives to the linguistic content? Now move your hands farther apart, but keep them at temple level and keep delivering the statement as you move your hands farther away from each other and gesticulate within the boundaries of this plane of gesture (eye and temple level). Can you feel how agitated, distracted, and frankly crazy you get as you gesture with your hands at this horizontal height and further and further apart? Of course, any audience would be joining you in this mental craziness because, as you learned earlier, people are all designed to copy; if they are not copying, they will be getting themselves mentally and physically as far away from you as possible, feeling too unsafe around this quality of movement and the unhinged mentality into which they presume it fits.

Now see what happens as you bring your hands in toward the center of this GesturePlane and give this statement with the fingers of both hands together at the top of the bridge of your nose—right at the center of this GesturePlane. Can you feel how mentally decided and assured you now are as you give this statement?

The area at eye level I call the GesturePlane of *thought*. Gesturing in this plane with the hands wide apart gives a feeling of the mind's being split and undecided, and this instantly creates stress in both your mind and that of any audience. As your hands travel in toward the center of this Gesture-Plane, the mind becomes more focused on one point, and there is a feeling of decision both in you and in anyone seeing and reacting to this gesture.

At this point in our investigation let's move our focus from the horizontal to a vertical plane that splits us right up the middle.

The WheelPlane

The center line of the body can be called the *WheelPlane*; it is an imagined line where the body is dissected symmetrically down the vertical center. (Anatomically, this is known as the *Sagittal* Plane or *Median* Plane, and it divides the body into the *sinister* and *dexter*—left and right—portions.) Gestures along the center of the body or the WheelPlane feel very decided when they are placed at the horizontal height of the ThoughtPlane of thought.

If you also understand that modern neuroscience suggests that one side of our brain deals in cognitive processes and the other side deals in creative processes, you can see how symmetrical gestures out from the ThoughtPlane can split the cognitive and creative brain, and gestures to the center can cause them to synchronize. You will also find that if you gesture in the plane of thought with both hands to the left of the WheelPlane, it has a very different feeling from when you gesture to the right. For most people, if you place your right hand to your temple and proceed to recount some tricky multiplication tables, you will make the task easier than if you placed your left hand to your temple. And when you place your left hand to your temple and imagine a great day on a lovely beach, this exercise will be far less tedious and infinitely more pleasant than it is with your right hand to your right temple: this hand placement will give a much fuller and creative visualization. Each side of your body is connected to the opposite side of the brain, and for most people, the right hand is connected to the left brain and cognitive thought, whereas the left side of the body is connected to the right brain and creative thought.

Using this knowledge when speaking to an audience is really quite complex, but movement based on the knowledge of embodied cognition can be used to initiate certain styles of thinking. More on this in the next chapter.

Over Your Head

Start with your hands touching the top of your head, then raise them up into the air high above your head as you say the following speech: "I have given the board all the information we have on this matter." Now try the same speech again while throwing your hands high above your head and sustain your gestures there.

All right—calm down now!

You were just then in the horizontal gesture plane that I call *ecstasy*. You can quickly experience the heights to which your energy can rise when you gesture with your hands above your head (see Figure 6.1). This is a plane that we may associate with the evangelistic speaker or the most highly charged "motivational" speaker. It's not for most of the business world's day-to-day communication delivery (unless you work on the floor of a stock exchange) because the energy of an average business situation rarely rises, either mentally or physically, to the level of the ecstatic. Even if business really is *ecstatically* fantastic, most people would suppress a feeling of total ecstasy because it takes us to a place over which we have very little control. It might be fitting for the high-energy business speaker who is motivating a thousand people at a keynote speech to really hammer home the message. But for the day-to-day office talk, or even the company pep talk, it could just look as mad as a box of frogs. Within the world of business body language, we see the EcstaticPlane used mostly to suppress extreme feelings — as with the hands covering the top of the head to suppress the feeling of "I'm mad as hell, and I'm not going to take it anymore!"

Most seasoned business communicators will recognize that voicing your thoughts with your hands high in the EcstaticPlane can easily result in your being escorted from the premises by security, with an offsite exit interview conducted the next working day. Business is evolving daily, but it is probably not quite ready to value daily ecstatic outbursts from the workforce in any positive way.

You have been warned.

So you can see that the head area alone has three distinct universal planes of gesture split down the centre by the WheelPlane and each section with its own distinct meaning and uses. And all of this before we look into the intricacies of the myriad of expressions within the face itself. So now that

Figure 6.1 Gestures in the EcstaticPlane

we have some understanding of the wider gestural frame for the face, let's look at some detailed expressions within the face, and learn about the most universal gesture to give from your head area in order to win trust and influence those around you.

Lie to Me

At this point, we need to revisit Dr. Ekman's (1972) conclusion that the emotions and facial expressions of anger, disgust, fear, joy, sadness, and surprise are biologically universal to all humans, and that these feelings cannot be hidden as they flash across the face to tell of the psychological state within.

But before we take a look at what these facial expressions are, let's first do a test to see how good you are at spotting their emotional triggers. Look at each picture of a face in Figure 6.2; these have been simplified to show only the salient points on the face that are needed for spotting six of Ekman's archetypal feelings that are encoded in facial muscles. Write down below each picture the feeling that you see, and then turn to the next page and check whether you spotted them correctly.

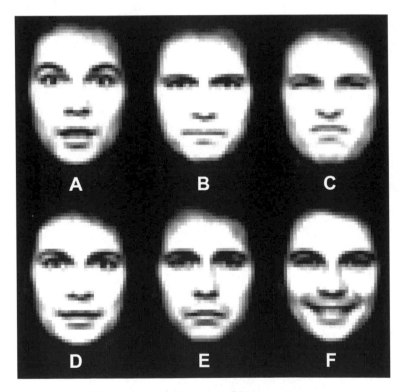

Figure 6.2 Six Universal Emotional Expressions

Here are the answers:

A: Surprise

B: Anger

C: Disgust

D: Fear

E: Sadness

F: Joy

How well did you do?

Even if you did well in this very simplified test of reading facial language, you will understand from earlier discussions that consciously using Ekman's knowledge to read others is full of potential pitfalls because of our equally universal human ability, skill, and often habit of (or in some cases sheer delight in) being duplicitous.

The Indeterminate Smile

What the master of business body language needs is to be able to produce an indicator of acceptance in the face so that the audience feels invited into the communication. Once again, art has an answer, and it exists within a thing called the *indeterminate smile.*

Take a look at Figure 6.3 and see how it affects you.

How do you feel when you look at this lip line? Do you feel yourself mirroring it and mirror-

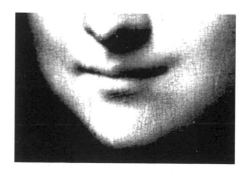

Figure 6.3 Indeterminate Smile

ing the feeling(s) with which it is encoded? Can you feel how you are invited in by this image of the slightly upturned lips, and even given a feeling that "something is *about* to happen"?

It is, of course, the smile of the *Mona Lisa,* and this smile has had an enigmatic hold on people for centuries. But the master, Renaissance visual artist Leonardo da Vinci, was not the first great artist to understand how the indeterminate smile (one that feels as if it could move to any feeling—laugh or cry or become angry or fearful) has a hold on human beings, drawing them into the face and giving them a sense of acceptance. Take a look at Figure 6.4.

Again notice from the shape of the mouth that the person shown here is not quite smiling, yet the mouth is positive and inviting. Again, copy or mirror the shape of this mouth and begin to see how you feel with your face muscles in this indeterminate smile position—*the edges of the lips just slightly turned up in symmetry.*

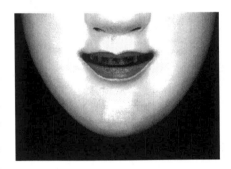

Figure 6.4 Ko-omote Smile

Laugh or Cry This slight smile is the facial key to inviting an audience to listen to you because, just as with Leonardo da Vinci's *Mona Lisa* smile, the smile on Ko-omote varies depending on the viewer's imagination or state of mind. The smile is positive enough to invite a viewer toward it with a feeling that he will be accepted, yet indeterminate enough that the viewer easily projects many of his own feelings onto the face of the communicator (the mask)—again to feel accepted.

In short, an indeterminate smile invites the members of an audience to look into themselves, and there is nothing that humans like more than seeing and examining themselves! As a presenter, when you use an indeterminate smile, the audience can feel more a part of you.

Here are the clear signals that we look for in the face to feel that we are accepted, and that, if portrayed confidently, will help to provide an atmosphere that will draw in an audience of one or many:

1. *A gentle smile.* This means that not only do the sides of the lips need to be upturned just a little, but the muscles around the eyes must also be congruent with the feeling. We can tell when the smile is "put on" or there is no smile *behind the smile* — in other words, when the intention in the mind is not congruent with the expression. You can use the in breath to achieve an inspired state that also opens up the eyes and gives congruence with a gentle smile.

2. *The eyebrows slightly raised.* This is the universal gesture of "I recognize you!" Every time we see someone that we know or that we are accepting, our eyebrows "flash," i.e., they rise up a little very quickly. Therefore, if you keep your eyebrows very slightly raised, not only does this open up your eyes so that your listeners can see more of them and feel that they can trust you more because they are "seeing the white of your eyes," but it also lets them feel that you have recognized them or accepted them alongside you. You will notice that this gesture does not tend to happen with anyone who has had Botox injected into the forehead. So the facial expressions (or lack thereof) of someone you know can suddenly become quite disturbing the first time you see her with Botox because there are none of the unconscious signals that she has recognized and accepted you. Such people often look as if they have lost their memory of you, although they are talking with you quite normally. Very weird, especially if it is your best friend or mother!

3. ***The head tilted slightly to one side.*** This gives your audience the "I'm listening to you" signal even when you are doing the talking. The head to one side is a universal gesture of *giving the other person an ear*. It displays the ears to clearly show that you are inputting information from them. You will also notice that tilting your head to one side feels very different from tilting it to the other. For many people, when they tilt their head over to the left, they get the furrowed brow of thought or questioning, because it sparks up their cognitive brain. And when they tilt it over to the right, there is a lighter feeling as the more open, creative brain is sparked into action. Try this out for yourself, with the knowledge that displaying either ear shows a level of engagement with your audience. Bear in mind that a long-lasting or perhaps exaggerated tilt gives a strong feeling of empathy from the communicator, and of course we mirror this, too. It does not, as some nonverbal communication commentators suggest, cause you to look subservient or give you a perceived drop in status. (At least only if you don't view listening to others and having feeling for what they say, beneath your level.)

Moving Ahead

This chapter has looked at the potential positive and negative messages that are created by the face, and created by gestures around the head area, and how you can use gestures in and around the head to get your point across effectively and change the way others relate to you and so move toward you. You are learning that the head area is extremely complex when it comes to body language. So as a skilled communicator with expertise in nonverbal body language, you should always be looking for clarity and not complexity in this and all other areas. To help distill out any complexity that has you confused and could confuse your audience, keep on reading!

Chapter 6 Quick Study

Gestures around the head and face are extremely complex, whether they are gestures of the hands around the face or facial gestures themselves. Humans need visual clues to what is being said verbally. We not only read *expressions* in the face to gauge emotional context, but also lip-read to better understand the verbal language. A raise of the eyebrows shows others they are recognized. The mouth is also most important for inviting other human beings toward us with a simple smile. A tilt of the head show you are listening and creates a sense of empathy and gesturing wildly with your hands above your head should maybe be saved exclusively for the day your office lottery pool wins the jackpot!

Just Do This Now

1. Keep your hand gestures away from your face in order to allow your audience to see your face, giving it the ability to better understand your communication.

2. Practice presenting on the in breath to help form the gentle "indeterminate" smile, encouraging the eyebrows to rise very slightly.

3. Practice "giving an ear" to others when you are speaking with them through a gentle head tilt to one side (for most people, it's preferable to tilt over to the right to show that you are actively and openly listening).

Chapter 6 Case Study

Theory to Practice: Careful

"Everyone knew that our senior vice president was working with a coach, but that did not seem like such a big deal. What started to draw our attention was when we all began to notice the same thing," explains Arthur. Apparently the combination of a corporate edict for more face-to-face meetings and some coaching advice—badly given or ill received—created an ongoing office joke.

"At least five or six times in a conversation, she would raise her eyebrows like this." Chuckling, Arthur opens his eyes as wide as he can. "It stopped after a while. I am not sure if or how it got back to her, but now, all you have to do is this (repeats eyebrow raise) to get a laugh from our team."

Insight

It is true that raising one's eyebrows shows recognition, which can foster trust and reciprocation. More specifically, the gesture is a literal "eyebrow flash." This anecdote is consistent with the adage that "a little learning is a dangerous thing." Subtlety is required in using any of these techniques. They are definitely tools, but you cannot wield them like jackhammers.

Provocation

What have others told you about body language that is now beginning to feel as though it could be untrue? What are you starting to recognize as a new truth?

7

From Complex to Clear Body Language

Clarity, Clarity, Clarity

Simplicity is the ultimate sophistication.
—Leonardo da Vinci

In this chapter you'll learn:

- Simplified body language for maximum effect
- What part of your brain is nonverbal
- The symmetry of powerful body language
- The secret of animal attraction
- How to confuse, obfuscate, and totally bamboozle with your body

I t is the same with body language as it is with actual speech: the more complex the communication gets, the more likely we are to either misinterpret the message or have to "tune out" in order to stay sane. So the question, then, is: how does one deliver more complex messages without confusing the audience?

In this chapter, we will be taking a look at ways to display simple body language that will support and provide the foundation for *a more complex message*. In addition, we will look at how you can use confusing body language to your advantage.

First, let's get some things clear about the complexity of the human brain.

Use Your Head

How many brains do you have? This is pretty easy to answer . . . you have only one brain. However, according to the research of Roger Sperry, a Nobel Prize–winning neuropsychologist, the cerebral hemispheres are divided right down the middle into a right hemisphere and a left hemisphere. Each hemisphere appears to be specialized for some specific behaviors (as was briefly stated in the last chapter and will be looked at in more detail now). Indeed, Sperry's findings are that both the left and the right hemispheres can be simultaneously involved in different, even mutually conflicting, mental experiences. But how does this play out in the body, and what is the benefit for business communication and winning body language?

Handy

Take a walk around any organization, and you'll find most people (about 90 percent) are right-handed or "right-hand dominant"—they prefer to use their right hand to write, eat, and throw balls of paper into the wastebasket. Most of the other 10 percent of the population is left-handed or "left-hand dominant." There are very few people who use both hands equally, known as "ambidextrous." In fact, most people also have a dominant *eye* that they use to "sight" or target something by closing one eye, using the open one to align a near object with it. Similarly, the dominant *ear* is the one that they prefer to use over the other. It's often the one that they cup a hand behind when they want to listen really carefully, feel that they have misheard, or are asking for verbal clarification.

Deconstruct

Working around the world and within many different cultures, I've had cause to think about and explore the universal structure and meaning of movement. Since my early studies I have drawn diagrams of the body and split it into sections, thinking and questioning myself about how to define the meaning of gestures in each of those sections, and how to combine those definitions to get the results that you needed from your body, your mind, and the audience. Take the arm, from the shoulder to the ends of the fingers: "What does movement of the fingers mean? Perhaps intelligence? What about the wrist? Imagination? The elbow—notion? The shoulder—involvement; the core: action?" My new models have evolved from older ones by masters of applied psychology of movement such as Rudolf Laban and his protégé, the great acting trainer to amongst others Sean Connery, Pierce Brosnan, and Anthony Hopkins; Yat Malmgrem. Over time, I have worked on distilling my ideas down to the ones you find described today in this book—the simplest and most effective models for nonverbal business communication.

Congruence of Movement

For a message that you send to stand the optimum chance of being interpreted correctly by the audience, it must be taken in coherently by both the left brain's linguistic logic and the right brain's nonverbal image processor. This means gesturing with more symmetry between the left side and the right side of the body. An asymmetrical gesture stands a very good chance of causing a cognitive dissonance between audience members' left and right brain, especially when they are trying to comprehend the language by both listening and focusing on the movement of the speaker's lips. As seen in Figure 7.1, a symmetrical gesture can lead the eye more easily and quickly to the mouth. It creates a focal point at the head area of the body. Constant symmetry also means less difference between the two sides of the body, and so an increased ability for viewers to predict the outcomes of behavior. Thus symmetry feels safer.

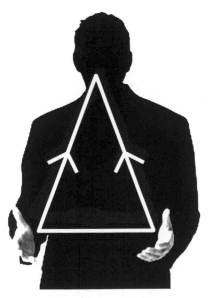

Figure 7.1 A Focal Point of Symmetrical Gesture

The more congruence there is between the gestures on both the left and the right side of the body and any words that are being spoken, the less chance there is of misinterpretation, confusion, or cognitive dissonance. For example, if you stand and place your hands symmetrically in the TruthPlane and say the words, "You can trust me," notice how steadfast and confident you appear, sound, and feel. Now place one hand in the PassionPlane and the other in the GrotesquePlane and notice a decrease in credibility, physically, vocally, and psychologically, when you again say, "You can trust me."

Let's test this out further on someone close by.

To experience for yourself the amount of confusion that you can create by using asymmetrical gestures (different gestures on the two sides of your body) that have no relation to your words, you are first going to find someone to talk with. Look around, pretty much anyone will do. As you talk with this person, make sure that your right and left hands are consistently at different horizontal levels. Furthermore, find as many moments as you can to change those horizontal levels. During this exercise, your hands should never be at the same horizontal GesturePlane. As you gesticulate in this way, see what happens to the expression on the face of the person to whom you are talking. Notice how he relates to you both physically and verbally as a strong indicator of how well he understands the content that you are exchanging with him.

Because you have been constantly changing your gestures yet also keeping them asymmetrical, a huge amount of dissonance is created for your listener. No doubt you will have witnessed this confusion for yourself. Indeed, some of you will have noticed that the person with whom you were speaking actually took a step further away from you (potentially showing an avoidance response), and in some cases will have found a reason to exit from the conversation entirely. It is uncomfortable to be on the receiving end of a speaker who is using incongruent and asymmetrical gestures. However, not only is symmetry simpler and easier to understand in the body, but it also appears that humans prefer it and are more attracted to it.

Classical Beauty. Plato, understanding that symmetry is attractive to the human eye, wrote of the "golden proportions" in the human face: the width of an ideal face would be two-thirds its length, while the nose would be no longer than the distance between the eyes. Today, certain proportional ratios have been scientifically proven to be inherently attractive to the human eye along with symmetry between the left and right sides of the face.

Award-winning psychological researcher Dr. David Perrett of St. Andrews University, Scotland, now believes that symmetry is the secret to how we are attracted to form. Studies have shown that babies will spend more time staring at pictures of symmetrical individuals than they will at photos of asymmetrical ones. Among adults, it has been shown that when several faces are averaged to create a composite, thus covering up the asymmetries that any one individual may have, these composite faces are deemed more attractive by more people.

Numerous scientists in the field of biology have found that the preference for symmetry is a highly evolved trait that is seen in many different animals. Females from swallows to swordtail fish, for example, prefer males with more symmetrical tails. The bottom line is that research shows that beauty matters — just look at any magazine stand and the number of beauty magazines that are on offer. It is no secret that beauty in all its manifestations pervades society and affects how we engage with one another. Bearing in mind the impact of symmetry on how we are perceived, we can help an audience perceive us at our most "attractive" by practicing symmetry in the body when communicating, giving us a true business advantage. And if, for any reason, you should ever wish to be off-putting with your body language, go for asymmetry.

Silent

As a theatrical consultant in movement for theatre companies worldwide, I have often worked with groups performing in languages other than English (which is the only language in which I am able to hold a credible conversation). Sometimes the languages have no relation to the English, French, Latin, or German that I might recognize, so I have no understanding of the verbal content of the work. What a gift—it means I can concentrate entirely on the story that the *action* is telling me. Often I might stop rehearsals and say, "I don't get it. . . . I'm lost. I can't see what is happening here!" The director explains the text or the plot or the emotional journey to me in English, and it is my job to add in what had been missing in the nonverbal action to tell me (and thus any audience) this. The result is theater that can be understood at a visceral level, leaving the mind free to really listen and understand the complexities of the text—a much better audience experience. Even now, I often work with my fingers plugging my ears or the sound turned down on video playback when I am helping speakers, those making TV appearances, or business presenters and politicians. That way, I can choose to concentrate solely on the movement and the feeling it will be giving to an audience.

Dissuasion

Here's an effective way to see how asymmetrical body language can work to your advantage when you are communicating. Imagine that during a presentation, when you are talking about your competitors, you are using positive speech but asymmetrical gestures. You can add some very complex gestures, both asymmetrical and shifting across all the horizontal and vertical planes of gesture. How does using this asymmetrical and complex nonverbal language make *you* feel about the credibility of the competition? If you want your audience to steer away from the competition and go with your business, even though you may be using positive verbal language, you won't be "selling it" for your competitors—you will, in fact, be creating a feeling of confusion around their offering.

Now imagine that when you are talking about the product or service that you are promoting right now, you switch your body language to symmetrical gestures in the TruthPlane. Can you feel how your content is elevated above that of the competition in the minds of your audience, although you were using complimentary verbal language while discussing both? By using asymmetrical and complex gestures, you can easily cause dissonance around content that you want to devalue in the audience's mind, and by using simple symmetrical gestures, you can promote ideas in an audience's mind.

Notice that the further the gestures depart from each other on a horizontal level, the more extreme the dissonance gets until it can easily begin to look quite unbusinesslike, unprofessional, and too bizarre for almost any office setting (see Figure 7.2).

Although there is no doubt that wildly asymmetrical gestures can have a certain attractiveness and sense of adventure to them, for the world of business, they are less bankable. So in the next chapter we are going to look at how to be not only simpler but even more focused with your mastery of nonverbal communication in order to bring you the results that you desire.

Chapter 7 Quick Study

Gestures with bilateral symmetry are easier to watch and read, and are perceived as more attractive. As a result, symmetrical gestures are more pow-

Figure 7.2 Asymmetry in the Body

erful than asymmetrical gestures, which can cause dissonance between the right- and left-brain functions in your audience.

Just Do This Now

1. Keep your gestures bilaterally symmetrical. You'll be easier to understand and, strangely enough, perceived as better looking and as such statistically have more potential for success!

2. Use asymmetrical gestures to add tension to a communication.

3. Gesture asymmetrically up and down your body to totally baffle and confuse any audience.

Chapter 7 Case Study

Theory to Practice: Asymmetry Is Ugly

Tina is in a difficult position. She has been given the task of delivering options for changing the procurement procedures for her region. Her boss has been very clear that she wants options, not recommendations. Tina has been thorough in getting input from everyone whose support will be required for success. Option A is clearly the best.

In presenting this option earlier, Tina feels that she was not able to clearly articulate the advantages. The delay came from her boss asking for a reevaluation of option A against options B and C. Further delay will be frustrating for everyone.

Insight

Instead of trying to add support to one argument, you can actually reduce the attractiveness of the other arguments. If Tina were to consciously bring asymmetrical and confusing body language into her description of options B and C, her boss would see those as being less attractive, and would be likely to gravitate to option A as a result of its being presented symmetrically in the TruthPlane.

Note: As with all tools and techniques for influence, the user assumes an ethical responsibility.

Provocation

When is it acceptable to use powerful nonverbal influence and persuasion techniques, and when is it totally unacceptable?

Directing the Pull of Your Presence

Focus Is Magnetic

People do not lack strength, they lack will.

—Victor Hugo

In this chapter you'll learn:

- The secret behind the secret
- Tribal patterns to present by
- Evolutionary influence techniques
- Magnetic mind control for business communicators
- Imaginative forms for physical messaging

Have you ever wondered how your body language can help you to succeed in a business situation? You must have done so at one point, or you wouldn't be reading this book. Anyway, some say a way to win is by influencing the agenda of those around you. Just as you can set a verbal agenda for a meeting, you can also silently set a nonverbal agenda with your action items at the top and ensure that people conform to it through your influence. So, right now, we are going to look at exactly how you can become a genius at *making your presence felt* every time you communicate and drawing people toward the outcomes you need.

An Open Secret

There are many books and courses out there at any given moment—right now, old and new—about how to attract whatever you desire in business toward you, be it anything from money to success or other people. Many of these books and courses have at their central core an idea that is often called the *law of attraction*. Simply put, this is the philosophy that people's own thoughts (both conscious and especially unconscious) dictate the reality of their lives, whether or not they're even aware of it. So, essentially the law of attraction says that if you really want something and you truly believe it's possible, you'll get it by directing your attention toward it. And if this is to be believed, then by the logic of the law of attraction, giving a lot of attention and thought to something that you *don't* want means that you'll get that, too!

The Unconscious Mind

The great psychologist Carl Jung, whose work was focused on creating a marriage between the conscious and unconscious elements of the human mind (introducing us to terms that are now commonly used in the psychological assessment arena, such as *introvert* and *extravert*), conveys through much of his work the idea that all human beings are connected together via a collective unconscious—"a reservoir of the experiences of our species."

This is, of course, most interesting to the seeker of business body language knowledge who already understands that the techniques within this book are designed from, and act upon, the unconscious mind through the use of images created by the physical body. You are, right now, exploring how to change people's minds using powerful pictures, or, as Jung might have classed them, *collective representations*. So let's explore more deeply the mechanics of the internal world and how images work in and on the mind—the *imagination*.

Imagination

Imagination is often thought of as the faculty of forming mental images or concepts of things that are not actually present to the senses. Yet, in fact, neurologically, the same part of your brain that is creating the picture of, say, the reality of this book and everything actually around you that you are seeing right now is the same part of your brain that creates any pictures that you might imagine, or indeed daydream or sleep dream. Understanding this puts a slightly different slant on how we might view reality and fantasy as different from each other, yes? And because imagination is fundamentally a facility through which we all make sense of the world, some evolutionary psychologists believe that it has allowed humankind to solve problems with a virtual reality system that is more than equal to reality itself. These incredible mental simulations of possibility have ultimately increased our fitness for survival.

Furthermore, the imagination has the ability to invent or entertain with the inspirational solutions it conjures up to the problems that were once considered unsolvable. The imagination is perpetually moving humankind forward. Breakthroughs in science and culture have often been born out of images created in the mind. Indeed, the word imagination itself is derived from the word *imago* meaning a perfect image. What if we were to play with the imagination, both our own and that of our audience, using universal images in order to make a strong connection between our own mind above and the body below, connecting both to our audience? What would these perfect images, these imagos, look like in terms of physical language?

Platonic Shapes

Plato is a good source for answers here when he talks about the theory of "Forms," which he does in formulating his solution to the problem of universals. The Forms, according to Plato, are archetypes of the things we see all around us.

To understand this a little better, let's think of it in this way: a Form is a perfect, objective, unchanging "blueprint." For example, suppose we have a triangle drawn on a chalkboard. The specifications for a perfect triangle is that it has three straight sides, with the ends meeting to create internal angles that, when combined, have a sum of 180°. The triangle on a chalkboard is far from perfect, so it is only our understanding of the *Form* "triangle" that allows us to know what the drawing is.

When we communicate through gesture, the more we try to bring ourselves toward the essential form of that gesture, the more we will describe an archetype that others can innately understand and be drawn toward. OK, so how do we find the essence?

The Form of Your Message

Pick an objective—what do you want from the communication or intend to happen out of it? Maybe you want a raise in status or in pay, or perhaps you want to sell double the number of units of product that a customer normally purchases or have the members of your staff cheer when you tell them the good news about this quarter's results. Think clearly of your outcome, and decide the action you should perform that will move you toward that outcome in the most direct way. Be sure not to clutter the goal you have set for yourself with other ideas or processes, and be sure not to muddy the action needed to get it with unnecessary movement. In short, keep this mantra:

Make a choice, make it bigger, and keep it tidy.

As an example of this idea, let's go back to our CFO and the "It's been a great year" speech. If this is the truth, and the CFO intends for us to understand that this is the truth, then why not just stay in the TruthPlane when delivering the message? Why do anything else? Why "change it up" or "give it some variety"? And when executing the plan why cloud it by mentally focusing on the intention behind the communication. Just perform it as physically planned, commit to the TruthPlane, focus on world outside and be available to change—action and reaction, just as in life. Now you are communicating naturally—authentically. Remember we don't walk around in life fixated on our intention (it is subconscious). For example, are you thinking about your intention behind reading this book as you read it? No, you are committed to the action of reading and reacting to what you read. The reason behind reading it is long gone from your conscious mind!

"Make a choice, make it bigger, and keep it tidy" means that you can make that physical language great enough to create an essence that consumes attention, and that very quickly your audience can mirror, empathize with, and will be drawn into.

Stage Fright

A business client came to me with the most severe case of stage fright that I've ever come across: whenever he presented, this person would break out in hives (swollen, red bumps on the skin, medically known as urticaria) all over his body. Even from quite a distance, the stress was quite obvious for all to see. Critically for my client, his superior in the company was using this stress reaction as a weapon against him, which was, I am sure, responsible to a considerable extent for exacerbating this acute symptom of extreme stress. (This kind of "leadership" is not uncommon, unfortunately, and only strengthens the theory that people don't quit their jobs—they quit their managers!) In just a single session with him I prescribed against the lengthy attempts of other performance "experts" to dispel this anxiety with repetitive positive thinking or affirmation, and instead asked my client to employ an attitude of complete acceptance of his anxiety around public speaking. We reframed the fear as quite normal for the situation, yet unhelpful on a professional level. With hands in the TruthPlane to not only countermeasure the physical effects of the anxiety, but also create an aura of calm, solid professionalism when speaking. The next day he gave a presentation hive-free! Not only this, but he now gives talks to mass audiences and he has moved ahead of his manager in the organization—as I expect was the fear that was at the heart of the bullying. (As a good friend of mine says, with more than a hint of sarcasm, "If you liked school, you'll love work!") In just about all cases of stage fright, battling the fear is never the answer. Accepting it is the first step forward. Bullying, however, is not acceptable. And you cannot bully the unconscious mind with relentless positive thinking, but as many great magicians have found you can reprogram it with archetypal symbols and action.

The Bottom Line

So now, using what we've learned, let's get right down to the age-old fundamental secret of physical persuasion and influence that causes others to move with you emotionally and mentally.

Be clear with your actions—and minds will follow.

Establish clarity in your movements based on your desires and objectives for communication. Then take control and focus your body—compared to the brain, it is a much larger organ, and it can quickly draw the minds of everyone around you into alignment. Remember: first we breathe; then we react; lastly (should there be enough oxygen left over), we think.

Once you have the will to control your body with enough clarity for it to be easily mirrored, your listeners are designed to "read your mind"; they will empathize with your desire and work with you to achieve it. You will copy each other—and people who are like people, like those people!

To reiterate an example that I've mentioned before, if you want your audience to get excited by your idea, well, get excited yourself. *Make the choice* to get emotionally involved, *make that choice bigger* (don't get a little bit excited—get *very* excited), and *keep it tidy* (don't add a splash of merriment or a hint of irony or an apathetic twist). Now decide on the movement to use with the audience. You could use the PassionPlane to create excitement in yourself. So make that choice and stick with it. Don't back out halfway and drop to the TruthPlane. Stay with the physicality you have pre-prepared to communicate to your audience as a symbol of your intention for the desired effect. In this way you take pure movement to the audience for the outcome you want and not mental intentions that will soon be lost from the conscious mind in the heat or anxiety of meeting them face to face—never making it to solid actions.

You can quickly form a "tribe," with your audience emulating *you* as the speaker, and emulating not just simple movement, but the vision that it represents. Though this focused, magnetic process of physical and emotional mimicry is technically primal and primitive, we are now well beyond the primates in how we can use it when we are communicating important messages—any monkey could copy another monkey reaching for a banana, but only a human, with our developed mirror neuron system and advanced right-brain imagery and metaphor system, can copy reaching for the stars.

Evolved Influence

Advanced understanding of the evolution of communication and our predisposition to learn through mirroring can help us understand how humankind's highest cultural talents are not nature but nurture. For humans, everything can be communicated, and therefore everything can be learned. That is why communication is of the utmost importance to humankind.

Your greatest business achievements will boil down not to a genetic disposition for success, but to your ability to handle the information that you give and receive in such a way that it is distilled into valuable meaning for other human beings: *intelligent communication.*

So in the next chapter, we will learn a fundamental vocabulary of pure movement with which you can meaningfully engage your audience.

Chapter 8 Quick Study

The most influential keys to the human mind are images that resonate universally, or archetypes. These are forms that we recognize as being connected to us, and toward which we naturally gravitate. The easiest way to get close to and master the art of communicating with archetypes is by making clear decisions about the outcomes you desire from a communication, and then decide and execute the biggest, simplest action repeatedly to achieve this outcome. Focusing on the outcome that you desire and then performing only the actions that will achieve that outcome is a route to the most direct form of communication.

Just Do This Now

1. Make a choice, make it bigger, and keep it tidy.

2. Decide what outcome you want from a communication, make that outcome even greater, and do not add any more outcomes.

3. Decide what you physically need to project to achieve that outcome, make that physicality bigger, and do nothing more.

Chapter 8 Case Study

Theory to Practice: Do One Thing Well

A recent shift in corporate strategy toward global teams creates an interesting situation for Erin in her salary negotiation. She has reported to her new boss for only five months, and she has never met him face to face. As part of the process, she has received 360-degree feedback on her performance over the past 12 months. Most of the areas of improvement speak to her lack of leadership in empowering others. She is fairly certain that this is a comment on her naturally flat demeanor.

She will be sitting down with her boss next week, while he is in town. Demonstrating passion may lead to a larger increase in salary. She is also aware of the fact that trust will be crucial to fostering a good working relationship with a remote boss. Can she show both sides at once?

Insight

The TruthPlane and the PassionPlane gesture areas send very different messages. In higher-risk situations, and with people who are relative beginners with these techniques, simplicity is always safest.

Erin could approach the meeting either way, but she will have more impact if she picks just one message—either trust me (TruthPlane) or see my energy (PassionPlane)—and executes consistently with that decision.

Provocation

What do you want? What can you do physically to get that? What would happen if you simply did that action to the exclusion of all else?

Holding Your Audience's Attention

Captivating and Compelling Rhythms of Movement

A child wants some kind of undisrupted routine . . .
a predictable, orderly world.

—Abraham Maslow

In this chapter you'll learn:

- The eight archetypal levels of tension and how to use them
- Why we get addicted to old routines
- How some communication "crashes" the brain
- Methods to hot-wire the mechanics of audience change
- Rhythms that turn brains on

How can you be entertaining with your body language in business? You don't need an arsenal of corporate knock-knock jokes to accomplish this feat—it's all about turning on the brain of each audience member, and it's easier than you think. The brain is a pattern-recognition machine that is constantly trying to predict the near future. It feeds on repetition, and it can handle a little bit of a surprise. However, the brain has a tough time handling several surprises in succession, or *unpredictability*. Of course, you may feel that there are many things you enjoy that are very unpredictable: action thrillers at the cinema, roller coasters at the theme park, and comedians at the club. Yet all of these are framed in the safe world of entertainment. The action thriller would be unbearable if it were real, the roller coaster would cause you to black out if it went on for more than a few minutes, and imagine spending a full day being told jokes by that comedian!

Repetition on the Brain

The simple and conservative use of neural resources is for a human being to seek out patterns or places that hold a certain amount of predictability. When the brain finds the familiar and the predictable, it does not have to keep gathering data, but can simply repeat the last set of data it received by predicting that there has been no change and using imagination to create an idea of the world. This mechanism has helped us and other advanced living organisms prosper by not having to use our time and resources gathering data on elements of our existence that are vital to our survival but that change infrequently; instead, we can shift our attention to opening up new frontiers. For example, when did you last check to make sure that your home had not disappeared? If you are not in it right now, then you can only imagine that it is still there. However (and most insurance underwriters will agree with me here), you are pretty well assured that it is still around (it's a low-risk item for just upping and leaving), which means that you can concentrate at work. Imagine sitting at your desk and thinking of your home, but having no imagination: "Oh, my! I have to go! My home has disappeared! I can't see it!" Thus, we are all to a lesser or greater extent creatures of habit, preferring to stay within boundaries that our imagination can safely predict within so that we can get on with advancing ourselves a little further.

Suffice it to say that our brain likes to know that the patterns that normally occur from moment to moment will not change considerably. We crave certainty, and this makes strong predictions preferable. In the absence of good, stable levels of positive prediction, the brain is called upon to use dramatically more of its resources on the simplest of tasks. Thus, humans seek out, move toward, and even reward stability and certainty. We avoid, retreat from, and often punish change and uncertainty—sometimes even just the *threat* of change.

One Fell Off

Here is an example that will illustrate this point further: when you perform the action of picking up an apple in a grocery store, the sensory system, sensing the position of the fingers at each moment, interacts dynamically with the motor cortex to determine *where* to move your fingers. Now, your fingers don't draw on fresh data each and every time you perform this action; you pick up an apple from the cart. The brain draws on the memory (plays past images) of what the apple is supposed to look, handle, and feel like in the hand, and this information is based upon expectations from, let's say, the last time you were in the market choosing fruit. No new data required; you are, as they say, on autopilot, almost sleepwalking in the supermarket.

But if the apple were to feel different from that last experience—perhaps it is moving in your hand with the rhythm of a small escaping rodent—you would immediately get a surprise and pay great attention. This unpredictability would be punished, perhaps by your dropping the apple and moving away from it quickly. Some people might shriek and climb into their shopping cart—and who can frankly blame them?

Although this is an extreme example, it nonetheless demonstrates that even a small amount of uncertainty can generate what we might call an error response in the brain. This sort of response takes one's attention away from one's goals, forcing one to pay attention to that error. For the business audience, it does not compute, or sit right, if something—or, more to the point, *someone*—is acting in a way that is incongruous with the particular backdrop of expectations. Some neuroscientists have likened this effect to having a flashing printer icon on your desktop when the paper is jammed—the flashing cannot be ignored, and until the problem is resolved, it is difficult to focus on other things. And so, in the case of business communication, your listeners cannot concentrate on your content, your strengths, and perhaps the nuances of your message (that is, really trust and understand you) if the part of the brain that generates the alarm is flashing an error message at them because they are not getting what they expected.

For many, the incongruity of, say, a business speaker's actions not sufficiently fitting his words can be so great that it almost generates what could amount to a "blue screen of death"—a fatal error (Mac users, don't be smug and pretend you don't have your own version of this!)—and the listeners shut down. They drift off and look elsewhere, or alternatively, they reach for something very predictable like their BlackBerry, which can be relied upon to report back "A" when you press "A"—highly predictable and thus now creating a sense of certainty and control for them.

Taking Cues from the Audience

Various forms of unconscious nonverbal communication from an audience, such as the use of handheld devices; the touching of hair, face, clothing, or objects; and drinking or eating, are good examples of potentially "self-soothing" actions—the desire to have sensory contact with and experience of something that is predictable and controllable. This is also an essential element of boredom—our minds switch off and disengage when we cannot connect with the experience, and we certainly cannot connect with anything that we cannot predict sufficiently within its context. This can happen when we are confronted in a meeting with, say, a communicator whose actions in no way fit her words. For example, she might say, "Let's all look up at this chart on the projector screen," while she herself is looking down at her laptop monitor, "You can all see what the figures mean," she says. Unfortunately, the listeners cannot see the figures, as they are too small, and therefore they have no idea of what the figures mean. So the brain searches for something it can connect with; seeing a bottle of water, the listener takes a sip, unconsciously thinking, "Looks like water and tastes like water . . . tastes like water again . . . tastes like water again," each time giving the brain a hit of its reward-for-recognition chemical dopamine, as opposed to thinking, "What is this person doing and saying? I can't understand it . . . the actions don't fit the content. . . how long will this continue?" and having the natural stimulant dopamine withdrawn as a punishment for being in an unpredictable environment. Self-soothing by the audience is often a result of being exposed to communication that is erratic, does not make sense, and is possibly incoherent.

Predictability and Change

Conversely, the act of creating a sense of certainty is rewarded in the brain, and examples are everywhere in daily life. Music is one such example, where simple repeating patterns enable us to fulfill our subconscious need to predict the flow of information, and in turn generate increased levels of dopamine in the brain—the reward response. The music turns your brain on, tunes you in to the content, and takes you away from (or mitigates) the effects of some of the unpredictability you were in before you heard it. Hence you put on your favorite music to calm you down.

Put simply:

Predictability is rewarded.

However, there is an evolutionary counterprinciple that brings tension to this:

Change is necessary.

And so the key question to answer is, how do you change an audience with an engaging surprise rather than a disengaging startle? What are the tensions that create fresh, engaging rhythms, and what are the tensions that create dissonance that repels? What is the rhythmic makeup of entertaining business body language that can win attention?

Framed

I've worked with a number of politicians at the highest levels of office, and elections are always the most interesting times for this work. You can see how the art of changing one's physical language can profoundly affect the way in which an audience of voters reacts to a verbal message. It is also a time when you can use body language strategically to destabilize the competition, say, in a debate scenario, by using specific gestures and rhythms that your opponents will follow, avoid or be compared against. This means, for me, not only studying the client's natural body language, but also knowing the idiosyncrasies of his opponent's movement when they are under stress and how they can be influenced to display this. I am not interested in the psychology of why they do what they do—only in how the movement looks to another human, and how that human is then liable to translate the meaning of that look and even mirror it or be repelled by it. So the work I do in these cases addresses how nonverbal communication can be used to high level strategic gain, and for political influence and persuasion beyond just the words.

It's All about the Rhythm

You should know that there is a huge difference between rhythmic and repetitive. A great beat is actually *rhythm*, rather than simple repetition. A repetitive beat has no change; it is thoroughly mechanical and engineered toward total accuracy and consistency. These are not inherently human traits (we are far more complex), and therefore human beings do not trust a simply repetitive beat as being genuine, whether it is the monotony of poorly written or produced music or the steady drone of a boorish CEO. We need to see a measured level of human inconsistency for a product, be it music or management, to *feel* natural rather than synthetic.

Rhythm has little skips, jumps, and suspensions in it that lend humanity to the beat and keep it alive. Great music has rhythm. Great poetry has rhythm. Great visual art has rhythm. Great dancers have rhythm. Great communicators know and use rhythm to engage their audience in their own heartbeat, life, and humanity.

So what is the archetypal vocabulary of rhythm in the human body, and how can we move with that rhythm in a way that engages the business audience? Even more to the point, how can we move with a rhythm that engages the audience with a predictability that is rewarding and which contains some surprises that are entertaining? We want to keep our audience on the edge of its collective seat, not falling from it in a narcoleptic stupor. Luckily, there are indeed rhythms that can help induce satisfaction, yet awaken people's senses further, and you are about to learn how to use these rhythms.

The Eight Archetypes of Physical Tension

The best way to use rhythm with an audience is through the eight clear archetypes of physical tension. All of these states of physical tension can be used as part of body language by the professional business presenter to engage, persuade, and influence the members of an audience—to change their bodies and so their minds. A good piece of entertainment, sport, or even a dinner party has an audience, spectators, and diners sitting in great anticipation at times. If there is sufficient *tension*—and by this we are talking literally about tension in the muscles—the participants don't get bored, look at their watches, or think about what else they could be doing.

All too often, the communications that we experience in the business context are not like this. Indeed (and unfortunately), it would not be unfair to suggest that more often than not, they are quite the opposite: tedious and enervating. So, what is it that we need to look at to make our physicality compelling and engaging?

When a communicator's body isn't "engaged," her whole content becomes saggy and turgid. On the flip side, when communicators are engaged physically, their communication is immediately more interesting. And that comes from engaging the muscles of the body in action. The audience's reaction is its engagement with the communication, caused by its mirroring of the clear tensions in the communicator's body (empathy with the speaker).

Now, of course, if the tension in the communicator's body constantly changes, then it is less possible for the audience to mirror this behavior, and so it will *lose attention* and empathy. If the audience members cannot discern *one clear* tension state in the communicator, then again, they can mirror only confusion. However, if you can simply and safely make a transition from one state of tension to another, your audience will follow. And so here are *the Eight Levels of Tension* that your muscles use: No Tension, Relaxed, Neutral, Deliberate, Alert, Agitated, Entranced, and Total Tension. Try them out on yourself for size.

1. No Tension

First, while you are sitting try to drop all tension from your body. Take away all muscle activity in every part of your body over which you have any control. Get as close as you possibly can to losing all rigidity in your muscle tone. You may begin to understand that this is the amount of physical tension that you have in your body when you are totally, totally relaxed, or even asleep. It is often called a catatonic state.

Slumped in your chair looking barely alive, you may suspect that this tension level is wrong for most business communication needs. Yet you also may be able to think of times when you've communicated in a business situation where parts of your body and mind or your audience have been close to this state at some level. If this is not what you want, then be sure to do and project something different. How about the next tension level up from this?

2. Relaxed

Now summon just enough tension in your body to be able to now stand or sit more upright, have a slightly straighter spine than in the first tension state, and get closer to holding your head upright. Your arms and your head should still be heavy, but you will find, if walking, that you are able to move in a fairly straight line, and so you'll find that your thinking is a little more focused. Some people liken this second state of physical tension to "walking in the heat" or to recovery from illness. Some feel that it is like being half asleep or having just awakened in the morning. It can also have a "laid back" or "cool" rhythm to it.

Again, imagine communicating one-on-one or to a larger audience with this physicality. Or even better, just act it out now and see the results you get in your vocal quality—pitch and cadence, rhythm and tone—along with the type of content and style that you naturally feel you want to present with your current tonality, musculature, and rhythm of body and mind. Maybe you need to be a little more laid back in some meetings, to take the pressure off and allow for more creative thought. But could this tension and rhythm in some circumstances also be unhelpful in persuading, influencing, or entertaining your audience, in drawing your listeners toward your content or simply communicating your trustworthiness as a professional?

If you are seeking to present a laid-back, casual manner and the laid-back thinking style that it provokes in you and an audience, then the relaxed tension state is certainly the one for you. Kick back and let the good times roll! But if your communication situation needs something a little more emotionally distant and factual, see if this next tension state could be useful for you.

3. Neutral

Now simply raise enough tension in your body to be physically "present." Use enough tension to hold in the muscles of your face and your whole body and sense the environment around you, yet also retain a modicum of relaxation. When you move your body toward a predetermined objective in this tension state, can you feel how economical your movement has become? It is almost as if you are pure movement: there is no past history behind your action, and so there is no remorse or pleasure and no excitement or pessimism concerning the action upon which you are about to embark. You are simply in the action for the sake of the action. You are strong, effective, and wholly economical. What happens when you speak using this tension state? What is played out within the rhythm and cadence of your vocal quality? What do you think is suggested by the rhythmic quality of your movement as it cuts through the space?

Some describe the feeling of performing in this tension state or viewing a person in it as being unemotional and detached, but quite powerful. It is also interesting to note that you can achieve this tension state by locating your centre of gravity at the dead centre of both your TablePlane, DoorPlane and WheelPlane as noted in the appendix. Now let's add an edge of energy to this.

4. Deliberate

Bring enough physical tension into the muscles of your legs, arms, upper and lower body, hands, and face to feel compelled to be slightly more forward in your action. Give yourself physical tasks to perform, and have enough tension in your body to create a feeling of wishing to complete the task. You should now have more internal feelings of satisfaction in your physical movement, and you should also be feeling a step-up in tempo from the neutral state. Certainly if you now compare the tempo, rhythm, and physical tension in this deliberate state to those in the catatonic and relaxed states, you will find how much more effective this tension level is for getting the job done.

Many people view this state as feeling very "normal" to them. Yet, judge now—how normal is this deliberate state? Do you function with a deliberate tension and rhythm for the majority of your day, and, more important for your work in presenting business body language, do you communicate in this tension state the majority of the time?

Do you sometimes slip into communication autopilot—a more neutral tension state, slightly detached from the action of the communication? At times have you communicated in a tension state of relaxation? If the answer is yes, was this a useful message to send to your receivers, or not? Now let's step up the tension to the "fifth gear."

5. Alert

By adding a further shift up in physical tension, you can move to a place where your senses are now wide awake, and you are, in turn, in control of your physical response to that stimulation. You may find that your mind is now inquisitive about what it senses and that your body is very much motivated to explore and push forward into space. You may find that you are cutting directly through the space to reach your objectives and complete tasks.

Imagine yourself right now presenting to an audience using this tension state and speaking with the rhythm that it gives you. How much does this feel to you like a powerful state of tension for your body and mind to be utilizing when you are communicating? It may feel like a little more tension than is ordinary—but then communicating to groups can be an extraordinary thing, and so a little "more-than-ordinary" energy in the body and mind may well be a good message to send, and necessary if you are to function at a more "peak-performance" level. Think about the rhythm of thinking that this tension state produces and how it may benefit your audience to think in this style. Now, let's push this further—perhaps too far, depending on what reaction you are trying to produce.

6. Agitated

Raise the tension across your body a further step up until you find that the objects around you are too much for you to encounter; you should have enough tension in your body that you feel you need to avoid coming into contact with the things in your environment. Increase the tension in your muscles until you find an edge of paranoia in your mind relating to the environment you are in, and even about your own thoughts and the movement of your own body.

Your body and your mind will feel more "held back" or "blocked" in this state. Some people have described this state as feeling as if their impulses are being stifled—"I want to move, but I can't." There is a great deal of strain in this tension state, and it is interesting to imagine or perform a communication in your workplace under the physical conditions and resulting rhythm that this agitated state presents to you and your audience.

How usual is this state in communicators? Well, I can bet that you see it and do it a great deal in business. How useful might it be for you to present this state to others and for them to mirror it and absorb it into themselves? It is certainly not relaxing, but as a positive, it could create a state of suspense in an audience, for example, and this would be great for keeping the audience engaged in moving on to the next thing you are about to say. Yet at more extreme levels, it could easily unnerve your listeners by being too chaotic and unpredictable, and the paranoia that this state produces will be unhelpful for many businesses. Yet not all high tensions are negative—so let's increase the tension.

7. Entranced

Put your body further into tension so that you now get a sense of being elevated and lifted off the ground and compelled to move forward. The tension in all your muscles should be very high, but not so high as to hinder your ability to move; although your tension has moved out of "agitated" and its chaotic rhythm, you will still feel unbalanced, but in a softer, more flowing way. This could feel blissful to you. You may feel as if you are in a rapturous state.

Now imagine communicating with another person or a group in this tension state. Do you ever communicate with others using elements of this tension state and its rhythm? Although it is quite extreme, have you ever seen others in this state, or communicating with elements or degrees of this state, and projecting this tension state from the movement of their body? This is the tension state that is embodied by the most evangelistic of business speakers. It projects an almost spiritual state. And it can certainly be used when you want to get across to an audience a message of quite awesome proportions—a new product launch or a huge merger that needs the physical performance of the message to be of epic proportions is a perfect customer for this tension state.

Finally, let's look at what happens with the maximum tension in your muscles.

8. Total Tension

Put your muscles into a state of total and complete tension—so tense that you simply cannot move any more, with every muscle in your body as contracted as you can possibly make it. Now imagine communicating with others from within this tension state.

While this tension state is extreme to the max, you can still appreciate how we all can often unwittingly incorporate an element of it into our communications. For example, imagine being caught out by a difficult question: your body freezes, and your brain locks. You fear that you do not have a clever, intelligent answer that correctly asserts your status in relation to the subject. Stuck now in this state of total tension, you can only deliver a short answer though your clenched teeth in an aggressive manner. You've lost your cool. This is also the tension state that can appear when we are extremely anxious. But given that you now know the other tension states that are available to you, you can more easily, quickly, and effectively shift to one that is more useful for the purpose of your message; just as with verbal vocabulary, having a greater physical vocabulary means that you have more options available to you, and so you are a more agile and powerful communicator. If you recognize that you are hitting a state of total tension, just shift, and take your audience with you. Learn to change your intention *physically* instead of mentally (as its derivation from the Latin implies: *tendere* —to stretch) and you are in command of your own psychology and of those around you by the fastest most direct route—the physical world of images.

Mnemonic

As a way to remember these tension states, name them easily, and so have further control over them as tools to use (or pitfalls to avoid), here they are listed alongside a couple of ways of describing their properties to help you remember this progressive sequence:

1. No tension: exhaustion, sleep

2. Relaxed: cool, casual

3. Neutral: economical, robotic

4. Deliberate: managerial, just-so

5. Alert: inquiring, is there a bomb?

6. Agitated: evasive, there is a bomb!

7. Entranced: blissful, in love with the bomb

8. Total tension: shock, the bomb has exploded!

Uses and Abuses of the Eight States of Tension

Having a fuller vocabulary of physical tension, you can now be more conscious of the tension that you use in your body when you are communicating. You can also use these tensions in getting what you want, given that your audience is designed to copy you. If you engage your audience with high tension, your listeners can become excited or anxious. If you engage them with low tension, they can become relaxed and even tired.

And, of course, you can move them from a relaxed attitude to an anxious one by using the higher tension states in communicating with them, just as you can calm them down by using the lower tension states.

By having more control of your own and so your audience's tension, you have more control of your listeners' attention and so their decision making.

For example, you can communicate in the cool tension state to gain rapport and so engender trust within a group that is casual toward your content. Now that you are all in sync, you can lead the group and build tension around the subject. This is an influence technique that is often referred to as "pacing and leading," where you first match the state where your audience is in order to gain mutual trust and then lead that state to where you want your audience to be.

Think how you can now approach an audience in the tension state of alert or "is there a bomb?" in order to provoke your listeners to inquire about the subject—to open up new categories in the mind from a tension state that gives a good level of in breath and so oxygen to the brain.

You can also lead an audience into a neutral state. This could propagate objective, calm, nonviolent communication—just the facts. And then, if you need to move the meeting on at a controlled yet industrious pace, you can shift up to the deliberate tension state, or a managerial "just-so" attitude: calm yet active; thoughtful yet productive; and steering well clear of the tension that could escalate into a feeling of "the bomb has exploded" and a meeting full of anger, fear, or just too much surprise to sit comfortably alongside. Now if you need to create meetings, presentations, and speeches that have everyone on the edge of his seat, waiting for the next person to get the chop and be fired on the spot, then for sure the tension of "there is a bomb in the room" is for you. Now you can start to think about the feeling that you wish to provoke when you communicate and pick the tension state that is going to get that feeling for you.

Moving the Feeling

Affecting emotions is very important to business communication. Feeling, you see, is partly in the way your body *feels*—the tonality within your very cells. If you want to move a person's feelings, you will need to move her physically, and now you have a clear map of the tensions that all of us humans can have and share together. You can see what might clash and what might click. If you are clear in displaying the map within your own body, your audience can drive to the destination—the intended feeling—with you. If you are unclear, then your audience will go its own way—and it is anybody's guess where that might be. It could certainly be in a direction that is totally opposite to the journey and destination that you had intended in the content of the communication.

But of course some people are "stuck in the mud" of their own feelings on a subject. So, too, are they stuck in the physicality that is a result of that feeling and opinion on any matter. For those in your audience whom you need to physically, emotionally, and intellectually shift, if they seem entrenched, it can seem to be totally impossible to move them on any level at all. Yet there is a most powerful technique of nonverbal communication that can move mountains, and it is coming up in the next chapter.

Chapter 9 Quick Study

Tension in the body is a great indicator to others of your intention. When others mirror that tension because it is clear, you have their attention. The rhythms in your nonverbal communication that are stimulated by the tension in your muscles are indicative to others of your psychological state, and also indicative of your engagement or disengagement with the matters at hand. You can therefore influence and persuade by moving yourself, and so your receivers, through different states of tension and into desired states of attention.

Just Do This Now

1. Relax your audience by relaxing.

2. Excite your audience by raising your own tension.

3. If your listeners are relaxed and you want them to be agitated, then join them in relaxation and start to move your tension slowly but clearly toward a higher state of tension in your body. Have a specific tension when you communicate to get specific attention from your receivers; choose the physical frame for your message, and in turn influence the mental attitude with which it is understood.

Chapter 9 Case Study

Theory to Practice: Tension Adjustments

The current work disruption is moving into its second month. Union and management representatives gather in a hotel meeting room for the weekend. The PR messages emanating from both camps assert: "This time we are serious." As the discussions push into the wee hours of the morning with few concessions from either side, tensions rise and tempers flare — but do they have to?

Insight

The common expectation of negotiations tactics is to increase the level of tension and cause the other party to "cave." Greater amounts of tension felt by individuals reduce their ability to evaluate alternatives and solve problems.

In any conversation, negotiation, or interaction, our tendency is to want to mirror the other person. Understanding the continuum of tension helps us control movements up and down on that continuum. The deliberate state is most effective for collaboration to solve complex problems. Consciously staying in (or quickly returning to) that state will bring the other person there with you. This may lead to more effective conversation.

It works the other way, too. Raise your level of tension, and you can find yourself in a very heated discussion, which may be exactly what you want to do.

Provocation

What is your intension right now?

All-Embracing Body Language

Influencing the Physical World with a Word

The art of acceptance is the art of making someone who has just done you
a small favor wish that he might have done you a greater one.
—Martin Luther King

In this chapter you'll learn:

- The number one thing that human beings desire
- Nonverbal influence in a word
- Body language that makes people stars
- A winning handshake
- Bad language that loses friends and alienates people

In business, the way we interpret patterns is sometimes the key to keeping our cool: the stock portfolio manager has (hopefully) seen some very consistent patterns of stability and growth in the market, whereas the client may see only relative chaos and inconsistency. So the manager sends out messages to calm the nerves of his clients, who are starting to feel that he is gambling with their finances. A simple chart presenting the value of the top 100 stocks over time shows the client that, on the whole, quite consistently the largest-valued companies keep on getting larger in value when judged over long periods of time—and so the client breathes a sigh of relief. This simplified picture of predictability hides the real day-by-day volatility of some stocks, a picture that would send the client back into a state of panic.

Investment

You will have discovered already that the currency of nonverbal communication has to have an overriding feeling of consistency, stability and thus certainty in order to attract an audience to connect with it and lead that audience to invest its time and energy with the communicator. We all move toward verbal language that speaks of stabilization or certainty. We also move toward any physicality that speaks of an association with these things: happy, healthy faces and bodies, for example, are seen as attractive to human beings. Many people who are seen as attractive know the secret that causes them to stand out in the crowd and attracts us to them. To understand that secret, first you must understand a very important concept that our brains link directly to our survival—*status*.

Status

This is about relative importance, the "pecking order," and seniority. In society, large groups, small groups, and even in one-on-one conversations, people have an idea of their status in relation to others. We are constantly sizing each other up and trying to determine where we stand, and this uncertainty affects our mental processes in many, many important ways.

Social hierarchy is a very logical system. The brain thinks about status using circuits similar to those that are used for processing numbers: our sense of status goes up when we feel that we are rated "more than" another person. When someone has this feeling of superiority, the brain's primary reward circuitry is activated, which once again increases dopamine levels—the key chemical component in the brain's pleasure and reward system. Japan's Department of Cerebral Research has shown that any increase in one's own perceived status produces a good feeling similar in strength to that produced by a financial windfall. And of course, on the flip side of this, the perception of a potential or real reduction in status can generate a strong threat response.

Tests using social rejection as a lever to cause the participants to lose status have shown, with electromagnetic resonance brain scanning technology, that such a reduction in one's status results in the same regions of the brain showing up as active as with physical pain. Thus, in business as in life, *being rejected literally hurts.*

Raising Other People's Status

We naturally and unconsciously move toward increasing our status and away from decreasing our status. So it stands to reason that if you could communicate nonverbally in such a way that you were able to increase another person's status at work, that person would unconsciously be attracted to you and your business message. Of course, this would also have to be done in such a way that your own status was not lowered—your unconscious mind would probably block you from committing any actions that might raise another's status at the cost of your.

So what if there were a way, a nonverbal technique, to raise another person's status without losing anything yourself—would you use it now? Well, good news: there is—and here it is:

Accept everything.

Let It In

How exactly do you "accept everything" with your body language, you might ask? Well, it is pretty simple, and the effects are astonishing. You must put yourself into what I call the *YesState*.

Remember, the human mind is naturally programmed to assign a negative perception to anything that is unknown. It's a primal survival mechanism. And this shows in your body language every second of the day when you come across an unknown entity—for example, somebody in business who is new to you or somebody who is known to you who has a new idea. Even somebody who is known to you and has a known idea that merely has some element of unpredictability about it will be met with some element of negativity. Instantly your brain goes, "Uh-oh! Oh, *no!*" and alerts you to a potential problem within the interaction, and this alarm frames the whole communication.

When you respond to an idea or a person in a way that gives you pause, your audience can see the elements of resistance in your body—you don't have to say anything (remember that potentially 55 percent of the feeling that people have about another person's intentions is based on what they see—and they can detect every tiny nuance of movement, tension, and rhythm in the other person's face and body unconsciously). When you are resistant to a new person or idea, that person can tell that something is wrong, but she is left to wonder what the problem is: is it the way she looks, her ideas, what she said, or how she carries herself? It does not really matter because your body language says that you don't accept her, and so there is an instant drop in her status. And a perceived drop in status will most likely cause her to either withdraw or attack.

Either way, at a subliminal level, you are no longer on ideal terms with your audience in the meeting, presentation, or speech. You've lost your listeners, or even worse, if you are compelled to be aggressive toward them, they now mirror that, and feel aggressive right back toward you. That is a result of what I call a *NoState*; this is our default state for most of the interactions that we ever have. It's not a bad thing—indeed, it saves our lives on a daily basis. But it does not move us forward; it is simply trying to keep us stable. It does not allow us to take an opportunity by dealing with the risk in an intelligent manner.

The YesState

In order to get into this nonverbal state of acceptance that can display a positive message to audiences of any size, we are going to take on a mental attitude of acceptance and positivity. However, there is no great psychological preparation for this, only to just now review as much positive verbal vocabulary as you can think of. Here is some to get you started:

Yes / okay / good / agreed / certainly / definitely / exactly / sure / true / yeah / totally / always / by all means / tell me more / you are right / of course / absolutely

---

As you read through this vocabulary, can you feel the difference that these words are making in your body? Can you feel how much more open you are becoming and the energy that you are now emanating? Spin the words slowly through your head and enjoy what they do to the feeling of tension and rhythm in your body. Do you feel more open now?

The accepting attitude of the YesState projects from the body by causing it to open up the belly and chest area to an audience, moving them full on to the audience to be seen. The belly tends to lengthen, creating a taller body figure and so increased status, yet vulnerability to the audience. This is a confident posture. The hands become more expressive and focus around the TruthPlane, and there is a gentle smile on the face and a gentle tilt to the head to show listening. The whole body is more compelled to move forward toward an audience and gain greater proximity and so potentially a greater level of intimate relationship (more on this important point in the next chapter).

Exercise: Walk the Self-Talk

Here's an exercise: take a walk around a public place with these words—a vocabulary of pure positivity—swimming around in your head. Make a decision to have these "yes" words as your inner monologue. Allow your internal voice to focus only on words that have positive associations of acceptance. Start with the word *yes* and then move on to as many others as you can; then just repeat the ones you like the most over and over in your head with no effort, because you need to pay attention to how others react to what they see. Remember, you are reciting these words silently, but notice how others look at you more, notice how others seem more drawn to you, and don't be surprised if you get stopped and asked for help or some such thing. Why? Because you now have the aura of someone who can deal with things! You look as if you are open and you won't rebuff or judge other human beings. You are now someone that people want to go to because you accept them—this is the YesState.

Reduce Your Threat

Why is this YesState so useful? Well, it can be surprisingly easy to threaten someone's sense of status accidentally. A status threat can occur through giving advice or instructions, or simply by suggesting that someone is slightly ineffective at a task. Many everyday conversations devolve into arguments that are driven by a status threat (the desire not to be perceived as less than another). When threatened, people may defend a position that doesn't make sense to avoid the perceived pain of a drop in status. For example, in most people's business lives, the question, "Can I offer you some feedback?" generates an emotional response similar to that evoked by hearing the footsteps of a potential attacker behind you at night.

Take performance reviews—the ninja warriors of corporate status ambush. Unless a person is 100 percent confident that he will be getting a perfect review, these evaluations are universally perceived as status threats. You, the manager, say, "This is just an informal chat about the excellent work you've been doing and *where you can improve*," and now the employee is lost in a fit of limbic-brain rage because the word *improve* implies that he is lacking in something, and is therefore lower in status than the people who happily possess the commodity he lacks. It frankly does not matter that you framed the lack, the "minus," with a "plus"; the brain still receives a message that suggests that it's now in a place where one of the fundamentals of survival, a stable status, could be dwindling. The person under review will either disengage to find the resource (status) elsewhere or fight you for yours.

Of course, you don't really have to say anything negative because you are communicating the message, for the most part, nonverbally: it is detectable in your body language and your tone of voice. In fact, it does not matter if you say only positive things because when the body sees the NoState or perceives negative nonverbal signs in or around any kind of performance review, it is immediately defined as a bad review—no matter what the verbal content of the review may be. Of course, the brain of the person under review had already NoStated the whole process in advance because he had no prior knowledge of what would be in the review—"If it cannot be predicted, it is bad."

Performance reviews can be ineffective at stimulating behavioral change no matter how you frame them because they are delivered with negative and closed body language. Many managers giving reviews say that they are extremely anxious and fearful about criticizing colleagues or, as they are often told to frame it, "offering areas for improvement." Those who are being reviewed pick up on the manager's anxiety and mirror it until very soon both parties spiral into a negative feedback loop. But if managers were able to give their reviews with a body language of acceptance, displaying open body language—with the torso and the belly unprotected by the arms and facing straight on, with the head tilted slightly to one side—then, even failure might seem to have some status and the review might be paid attention to. This does not mean that people are promoted when they are incompetent, only that they can now listen to the review because it *looks* less threatening to their status.

One scientific study showed activation of the reward circuitry in the brain when people were simply given positive *verbal* input—this occurred when participants were told the words "that's correct" by a repetitive computer voice. With the YesState, you don't have to verbalize the positive vocabulary, but only to let the internal positive vocabulary infect your nonverbal communication—which, as we've seen, is the communication that really counts when you are creating a feeling, positive or negative. And for anyone who fears that she will inadvertently give her workforce too much nonverbal praise, inspiring a parade of requests for promotion and increased pay, it is widely reported that because of the deeply rewarding nature of status, giving positive feedback may reduce the perceived need for a raise in salary.

Acceptance

The YesState will help you recognize that there is absolutely no downside to projecting a physicality of total acceptance to your audience. When your listeners first set eyes on you, their unconscious feeling should be, "I am wanted." From the very day we are all born, the thing we really need and even crave from others (once we have been fed) is the feeling of being *accepted* by them. To see in their faces and in their whole body that we have a positive place with them and that we are welcome is what we desire most. If you can give people that feeling, then you are truly an attractive human to be around, along with all that you say and stand for. Watch the Hollywood stars on the red carpet: total YesState (the open body language, gentle smile, and tilt of the head as the paparazzi fire off a hundred flashes in their face and ask a thousand crazy questions). The most gracious and starlike of them accept us, their audience, even when we invade their space in a quite brutal fashion, and we love them right back for it.

You too can use this brilliant technique when you feel you are being "attacked" in business. When information comes that seems like it is a slight on you or your work, keep in the YesState and accept the attack nonverbally by opening yourself up to it right into your vulnerable belly area—the TruthPlane. Nod your head and give a gentle smile, opening your eyes to all the information within that assault. Stay on the in breath and take your time to react as you need to in order to persuade and influence your assailant to a better point of view for him. You will be awed by how he nods his head at your points, and by mirroring your open body language back to you, quickly moves toward your side of things.

Some of you may recognize this technique as a physical one used in many ancient martial arts to manipulate and reapply the aggressors energy in a positive way.

Push and Pull

Probably the most effective gesture of acceptance is to pull something toward you, and the most effective gesture of rejection is to push something away. So if you make the gesture of *bringing your audience toward you* in the TruthPlane or the PassionPlane, people feel more accepted, and you indeed feel like you accept them more. Conversely, a *pushing-away gesture* will cause them to feel rejected and help you to feel as if you are rejecting them.

The cognitive results of these accepting and rejecting gestures were studied at the Center for Cognitive and Social Neuroscience in Chicago, and a definite preference was found for content associated with a pulling-in gesture. So speak and gesture toward you and you will show a preference for those to whom you are speaking, and they, in turn, will mirror a preference for you.

Bulls and Bear

Before working with the president of a very large trading organization, I was warned what a bear of a person he was, and that I should be ready for plenty of resistance, out-and-out aggression and not to be intimidated by his high level of intelligence. This is a warning that I routinely get from human capital departments when I am training high status individuals and teams often considered by their company to be the "brightest and the best of their kind anywhere in the world." These people always turn out to be fairly normal human beings when they are treated as such. I often move the halo effect around them to one side by asking if they remember the day that they became CEO, president, or premier, and how on that day they suddenly became the funniest, most intelligent person in the room and a speaker who can keep their organization enraptured. Yet overnight they had not managed to find a better understanding of comedy, they were down several million brain cells, and they had not assimilated any further conscious competence in public speaking in their sleep. Remember that when you get the office of power, you inherit many coercive levers that cause your organization to act brilliantly as if you are a great leader.

Anyhow, I met the big bear, and as I expected, he gave me a bone-crunching handshake. I immediately gave him the upper-hand handshake (I give you the training for this later in the chapter), while telling him what a good strong handshake he had, smiling all the time and nodding my head, accepting the potentially aggressive move by using the YesState. He, in turn, smiled immediately and nodded his head and relaxed, as I then told him to take a seat and began to insert instructions as to how his training with me would proceed. He was now under my influence. The big man just wanted to feel safe. However powerful anyone is, all he is looking for is acceptance.

The Upper Hand

Here's another great way to give others a huge sense of acceptance and status every time you meet them by using the time-honored greeting, pattern, and, for many, cultural norm of the handshake. You are now going to learn a piece of body language that causes anyone whose hand you shake to get a great sense of pleasure from being with you. First, let's look at the significance of the handshake gesture in our communication system — why it exists, what it does, and how that works.

History of the Handshake

Certainly within the majority of Western Hemisphere cultures, there is an age-old tradition of gripping right hand to right hand with another person that you meet; and in Eastern Hemisphere cultures there is a very prominent tradition of bowing. Now certainly, it is fair to say that both these traditions come from an understanding of hierarchy. In the bow, it is often traditional for the lower-status individual to take his head, and in some extreme cases his whole body, to a lower level than that used by the higher-status individual. This creates almost a horizontal depiction of the numerical status — a "bar graph" of hierarchy for everyone to see. Traditionally, in most Eastern sword cultures, this gesture had the extra "bonus" that whoever held his head in the higher position had a greater chance of chopping off the other's head first. Thus, the lower of the two would have been submissive to the point of putting his life at the mercy of those higher in the pecking order.

The handshake is a little more egalitarian in that by clasping their right hands together, both parties involved in the greeting instantly recognize that neither has a tool or a weapon in that hand — nothing dangerous is being concealed. Thus the handshake tends to be initiated once two people are in close enough proximity to each other that each can no longer see the feet of the other within the peripheral vision — i.e., they are so close that they are unable to both get eye contact and see foot movement and so are unable to compare the emotional information in the face to the information displayed by the feet concerning the larger intention of the body. For this reason, we look for more information from other parts of the body in order to predict what the other person's intention is and judge that against the look on her face and the words that she may be saying. Shaking hands is a perfect way to understand the possible intentions of another human being through the tension, rhythm, direction, resistance, heat, and moisture in the hand. In addition, the hands and arms are now much closer to striking distance, and so there is more threat of danger. Hence we have a ritual whereby we get to touch the other person—sense the energy in her skin (is she tense, aggressive, passive, calm, or feeling some other emotion?), and also notice if she does in fact have anything hidden in her hands that could harm us.

Disarming or Alarming

Although the handshake is egalitarian, this simple cultural norm is often used today to show dominance. Some people, for example, will give you (consciously or unconsciously) a "crushing" handshake in order to display their greater physical strength relative to yours. Other people will unconsciously employ a flaccid grip to give you the idea that you have more strength than they do—in other words, to demonstrate their submission. However, if during a handshake, either (or both) party does not get to feel the palm of the other's hand—i.e., if full contact is not made in the area of flesh between the thumb and the index finger of both parties, and so the palms also do not get good full contact—this instantly causes a reaction of movement away from the now potential threat.

In short, it is alarming not to feel the palm of the other person's hand in a handshake. Try it out with a friend or a good work colleague—it is most interesting with someone you know and trust fairly well, because when you shake hands with him you do not give him the palm of your hand, then you will notice a very quick change in his face, maybe even a universal facial display of disgust, fear, or even surprise. Even though the two of you know and trust each other to a higher degree than most, your unconscious mind, which is protecting you second by second, does not take this fact into account. Your unconscious mind perceives only that there is information that it does not have, and therefore it is unhappy—the result is "retreat, be cautious, or attack." So it is clear that to build trust, an effective handshake always gets good full contact palm to palm. And not only can you build trust with a handshake, but you can raise the status of another person without lowering your own. But first, what *not* to do.

Getting the Upper Hand

Even with good palm contact, it is possible to shake hands in such a way that you become dominant, thus lowering the other person's status and making her shut out your message: simply turn her hand slightly over during the handshake so that your palm is *on top* of hers. This gives you more control of her arm (it is easier to push your whole weight down on her arm and control it than for her to bring her weight and center of gravity upward to push up against gravity and your arm's strength). When you have the "upper hand" in a handshake, you put the other party at a physical disadvantage. You have "one-upped" her, her status is lowered, and now she is fleeing or fighting you. Try this with a friend or colleague and see what happens, both in her facial expression and in her full body language. Do you notice the aggression (locked eye contact, squaring off of the shoulders, and so on)? Or do you see her become passive (dropping eye contact and lowering her head, along with some folding in at the stomach and across the shoulders, and maybe even a step back)?

Also notice what happens if you push your upper hand along with your colleague's closer toward and nearly touching her stomach area—right into her TruthPlane, one of the most vulnerable areas of the body. Do you notice how she instantly becomes passive? Even if she might have been aggressive at first, once your hand moves into this very vulnerable area of the body, her unconscious mind knows that she has been compromised, and it will wait for further instructions from the higher-status individual. You could even now put your left hand on to her right elbow, taking control of her forearm. This handshake is almost as controlling as any "greeting" can get, and using it is the secret to losing friends and alienating people! Get someone to give you this handshake so that you can feel how bad it is to receive it, and by doing this, you'll stand a great chance of never, ever, accidentally or even purposely, doing it to anyone else. It should be reserved only for when you have such a great business that you wish to lose deals from the onset or when as a leader you have come to the realization that you are a master of the universe and all should quake in your presence!

Giving the Upper Hand

Of course, knowing all this, you can use the opposite version of this technique to give another person status. Doing so instantly raises his engagement with you because of the sheer unconscious pleasure it gives. What if every time you met someone, you could now make him feel like a million dollars? Here's all you have to do to make people feel that way: when you shake hands, simply turn the other person's hand quickly and gently so that it is slightly over yours, and at the same time quickly and gently move both your and his clasped hands closer toward and into your vulnerable stomach area (right at a level with the belly button—the TruthPlane).

Try this out and you are going to be truly astonished at how the corners of your handshake partner's mouth instantly turn up into a smile and he steps in toward you and makes great eye contact. He feels good with you and relaxes. And when he feels good with you, then everything around you, including the message you are giving him, is good.

Get Ahead

By now we have adequately covered the mirroring concept. When you have an audience, its members will more often than not begin to mirror your actions. Accept, then, and notice how others will mirror you and your accepting attitude—your YesState and all the body language that goes with it. For example, in the YesState, we are more predisposed to make nodding head movements up and down, which in Western business culture has the inference of positivity and agreement. When we are in the No-State, we are more inclined to shake our heads from side to side in what many would agree is a "no" gesture or has a negative inference.

In many cultures, the head nod is most commonly, but *not* universally, used to indicate agreement, acceptance, or acknowledgment. Different cultures assign some subtly different meanings to the gesture. However, nodding to indicate yes is widespread and appears in a large number of diverse cultural and linguistic groups. There are varying theories as to why nodding is so frequently used to mean yes. One simple idea is that it is a form of bowing, indicating that one is prepared to accept what another person is saying or requesting. It is also noted that babies, when hungry, search for their mother's milk by moving their heads vertically, causing them to suckle, but decline milk by turning their heads from side to side in the "no" head gesture to shake their mouths away from the source of food.

This is why the business body language expert is looking to *give* gestures of acceptance, not to search the room to see who is sending them out. The master of nonverbal persuasion uses his own powerful "yes" gestures to cause others to copy and mirror the accepting attitude, and so creates an atmosphere in which possibilities are opened up. The influencer then uses his communication to put forward the new options into the positive space.

Remember, great influence and persuasion has more to do with the messages that you know you are sending out than with the messages that you think you are getting back. To be plain: body language reading in business is for fools! (Or for the very, very expert, with a great deal of focus and time to assess all the variables.) Don't go there. Especially when you have such a capacity to influence others around you, reading body language is rather like trying to read the complex weather systems across the whole of the globe when all the time you are holding in your hand an instant global rainmaker! You must fully orchestrate your nonverbal message to fit the results that you are looking for. Therefore, you need to be able to work the entire room with your nonverbal communication — and that is why the next chapter is about how to create spaces that influence many bodies, causing them to interact together to your advantage and to their group benefit.

Chapter 10 Quick Study

The more you *accept others*, the more they are disposed to accept you and act in your favor.

Just Do This Now

1. Use the YesState. Think with positive vocabulary about everything you see and hear during a communication in order to accept it (not necessarily agree with it). This will create an overall nonverbal atmosphere of acceptance with open body language that invites others into you.

2. Use "pull" gestures frequently to confirm acceptance of others and acceptance for your content.

3. Give others the upper hand when greeting them with a handshake. Remember that people who give status and advantage to others are seen as having enough to give away.

Chapter 10 Case Study

Theory to Practice: It's All Good

The visiting workgroup from Japan is arriving for two days of meetings and greetings. You have been home and back to the airport twice because of the flight delays caused by the Pacific typhoon. You were supposed to be with your boss and the two integration project leads when you met the arriving group, but it is 2 a.m. and you are the only one who could make it to the airport to meet these people.

Your Tokyo office has contacted you, saying, "They can't wait to see the fall colors," and this hangs heavy in your head because a wet Indian summer has kept things lush and green. So much for the planned drive through the hills tomorrow afternoon!

As the five-person delegation approaches, a million questions erupt in your sleep-deprived mind: Do I shake hands or bow? Bow to the group? To individuals? In what order? Firm handshake or soft?

Nuggets of cross-cultural insight return to you:

- Don't be too overbearing; Japanese are more subdued.
- Smile, but don't show your teeth.
- Make small talk about the weather.
- Match their number of people in meetings whenever possible.

(Argh!!)

Insight

The most effective piece of insight for such situations, cross-cultural or not, is to relax and accept. Acceptance breeds acceptance. If you consciously think, "Yes, good," your body will relay that feeling, which will be returned by others.

- "Yes, he looks quite flustered, maybe a run-in with customs . . . that can happen."
- "I am here by myself to meet a very important group of clients . . . yes, indeed!"
- "Yes, we just had a confusing exchange regarding whether to bow or shake hands . . . OK."

The relaxation and acceptance will be apparent to others. In turn, they can relax and mirror acceptance back to you. Now everyone can take it easy and make connections.

Provocation

What is the most positive cross-cultural gesture for you to make?

Position Yourself for Success

Presence, Place, and Power

You can have power over people as long as you don't take everything from them.

—Alexander Solzhenitsyn

In this chapter you'll learn:

- How you can easily lose the advantage of territory
- When close is *too* close
- How to control Maslow's pyramid of needs
- The science of "faking it" for money
- How to gain intelligence by choosing the right seat

The idea of *territory* comes up quite often in thoughts, theories, and practices on nonverbal communication, and of course in business, so you could well be quite familiar with the idea already.

The idea of animal territories was most widely popularized by American anthropologist Robert Ardrey in the 1960s with his book *The Territorial Imperative*. Ardrey challenged previous assumptions about human development with a theory that a high level of territorial aggression was the fundamental characteristic that distinguished humans from their less aggressive primate ancestors, and consequently was the evolutionary catalyst to modern human beings. This theory influenced cultural icons such as Stanley Kubrick: it is obvious in Kubrick's film *2001: A Space Odyssey* (widely recognized as one of the best films ever made). In this work, the awakening of human intelligence is depicted as being the result of a violent act. Still today, there is much debate and theorizing regarding the relationship between the evolution of Paleolithic technology (the hand axe) and advances in human cognition. For example, recent research in evolutionary and developmental psychology hypothesizes that the extra neural mass essential for the dexterity required in manufacturing hand axes also supported early verbal language. This idea certainly helps substantiate the theory that humankind's advanced physical development as a response to surviving the environment, laid the ground for neurological developments allowing verbal language to eventually flourish.

Ardrey's influential work on aggressive territorial behavior and evolution can also be seen in the reptilian mindset of Oliver Stone's 1987 movie *Wall Street*, widely understood as a critique of capitalist excess. This idea is best expressed by Michael Douglas's character, Gordon Gekko, who claims, "Greed captures the essence of the evolutionary spirit." It is certainly no overestimation that territory is hugely important in business—as you would discover if you arrived at your place of work to find someone else sitting in your space, eating a snack, and looking through your files, uninvited and unannounced.

Territory around the Office

When we are under stress, we can easily stake a claim on whatever resources we believe to be ours (and maybe some that we merely think *should* and need to be ours). For a communicator using influential body language, it is essential to present a physicality to others that does not fire off a reaction in their brains telling them that their territory is being invaded. More often than not, you are looking to present an image that says, "I am here to offer you more resources or to bring back the resources that you have lost to others." Put simply, "I am here to feed you—not to feed *on* you and your territory."

Messages that will suggest that you are taking over include leaning on, touching, or standing in close proximity to another person's objects (which includes just about everything, such as fixtures, stationery, computer equipment, or furniture). Leaning against an object, while seemingly innocent enough, can be perceived by others as dominating and intimidating. To observe someone leaning against a wall, or hanging in a doorway or a passage, can make us feel that the person leaning is displaying an attitude of ownership over that exit, entry point, or pathway (Figure 11.1).

Often, if people do not *own* the property themselves, they will seek to own the pathways to the property, thus canceling out the benefit of ownership. What status can owning a place have if you can't get to it? It is the same for workplaces: hanging out at the water cooler, and so creating a territory around the vital resource of water and the social hub of the office, can at times be more powerful than sitting behind the president's desk—especially when the office air conditioning breaks down on a hot day, or if a widely viewed event, such as the Academy Awards or the Super Bowl, took place the previous night.

Figure 11.1 Territorial Display

Calm and Assertive

When you walk into someone else's territory, you are metaphorically walking on eggshells with potential land mines buried underneath. How do you deal with this? Once again, you must remain calm and assertive. Be sure that you feel centered in your belly area—balanced, with your hands and gestures open in the TruthPlane. You are looking to project an image that says that you can stand on your own two feet, and that you will not take any resources away from the other person. In short; when you move your own vulnerable center into the space, you are being assertive without being aggressive—something that is an immense relief to the other person, whether she realizes it or not.

There is, of course, a sense of relief when further basics of survival are supplied and respected while communicating; therefore, whoever has taken control of the provisions (food and drink) and the light and heat (air conditioning, blinds, or lighting) commands a great deal of status and so attention from others in the room. To be the provider of all the basics of sustaining life has a huge significance, drawing others toward you. What being in this role absolutely does *not* do (contrary to what others may believe) is take you down in status to the level of a subordinate servant. It can be a powerful thing to serve the coffee! Great leaders pour the drinks sometimes. John Maxwell, the multimillion-selling author of *The 21 Irrefutable Laws of Leadership*, says, "The measure of a leader is not the number of people who serve the leader, but the number of people served by the leader."

Maslow's Hierarchy of Needs

We can glean from this concept that the fundamentals of territorial behaviour center around the *basics of survival*, all of which are to be found right at the bottom of Maslow's Hierarchy of Needs, a representation of various types of needs that must be met in order for an individual to be happy and healthy. This theory was developed by American psychologist Abraham Maslow. Maslow is considered one of the fathers of twentieth-century humanistic psychology, and an innovator in psychological theories that diverged from Freud's ideas around "sickness" and the mind, focusing instead on *what human beings need* if they are to be healthy and happy.

Maslow saw the needs of humans as being arranged in tiers. The most basic needs, at the bottom, are physical—air, water, food, sleep, sex, and the basic bodily functions. In the next tier come safety needs—security and stability in areas such as health and property, employment, resources, and the family. In a still higher tier are psychological or social needs—for belonging, friendship, love, sexual intimacy, and acceptance. The penultimate level is the need for esteem—to feel achievement, status, responsibility, and reputation, or the respect of others. At the top of it all are the self-actualizing needs—the need to fulfil oneself, to become all that one is capable of becoming: acceptance, problem solving, creativity, and spontaneity. Maslow felt that unfulfilled needs in a lower tier would inhibit the person from moving to the next level. His illustration: "Someone dying of thirst quickly forgets their thirst when they have no oxygen."

We can apply this model and way of thinking to communication: someone whose territory is being invaded, with her status being potentially lowered or vital resources pilfered, is unable to listen effectively to your presentation on how she can grow her business more creatively. She cannot listen to your vision statement expansion if you just took her last and only pen to illustrate it. And a member of your staff may find it hard to listen to and respect your instructions if you are sitting on his desk, making a nonverbal claim on what little territory and space he may have as his own.

Establishing Your Territory in a Room

How you orient yourself and others within a room or around a table is vitally important to how comfortable everyone's own status is in the territory. Watch out for objects such as furniture and fixtures that create barriers between you and your audience. The classic example of this in business speaking is the podium, a throwback to a medieval castle where feudal leaders commanded the people from a safe and protected distance and height (because they feared the arrows and spears that the people wished to throw at them due to their autocratic rule!). The podium, for the modern-day speaker, denies the audience any visual or physical access to the speaker's whole body—especially the hands in the all-important TruthPlane and so can be a barrier to trust. This is true unless the podium has some sort of insignia at belly height, giving a symbolic social stamp of approval and status (the U.S. presidential podium is a good example, with the seal of office, the "eagle within stars," and the words "E Pluribus Unum" all placed at TruthPlane height to the speaker). In all other cases, the area that we trust the most is hidden from sight for no good reason. The audience cannot see any open hand gestures, unless they are over the top of the podium at chest height—and at this height, in the PassionPlane, the speaker is more likely to go over the top emotionally and become overly passionate or too direct. You should consider moving away from the podium into more open space, in order to show your openness to the crowd (both literally and metaphorically).

Also, if you are seated while you are giving a speech, pull your chair back from the desk or table and make sure that it is high enough so that you are communicating from your TruthPlane over the top of the table. This will relax the people in your audience: they now have access to your vulnerable stomach area, and you look confident. For a good example of communicating effectively while sitting behind a desk, just look at any news anchor. His desk is always set at a height such that the hard copy of the news sits on top of the desk, and consequently cuts directly in at his TruthPlane. Furthermore, his hands rest on the desk at belly height. There is no mistake or coincidence in this placement: the image we get is that the news reader is trustworthy and his news is *fact* and not simply subjective editorial opinions.

Born to Be Mild

I was once engaged by a prominent criminal defense lawyer as an expert witness in a conspiracy to murder trial involving an alleged criminal organization; I was to give my expert opinion on some video evidence that was being put forward as key evidence by the prosecution. Over two days of examination and cross-examination, I explained how the evidence clearly showed to me that the accused showed signs of extreme stress and was under duress. The defendant displayed clear signs of wanting his alleged co-conspirator (actually a paid police informant) off his territory. He was pacing up and down, avoiding eye contact, and constantly looking away from his home, gradually leading the police "plant" off the property; these were not the actions of two people who were "thick as thieves," but more of a victim and aggressor. In court and out of my usual territory, it took all my skill and technique not to fall into the traps set by the crown prosecutors through their relentless questioning that hoped to cause me to become anxious, aggressive, and destabilized. They knew that if they could cause me to lose my calm by badgering me for several hours non-stop, I might certainly lose some of my credibility with the court. Once again—simply holding my hands in the TruthPlane (quite a feat over two days, even for me) kept me confident and stable even though I was out of my element. The verdict came back not guilty.

Two's Company

The way people group together and the distances they maintain apart from each other are also extremely important for understanding and therefore engineering body language that drives others toward your goals. This is especially relevant when you are facilitating meetings, running brainstorming sessions, delivering training, or doing something similar.

The *number* of people who are in a room together, and how they are placed, will have a definite bearing on your comfort level in most situations. Notice how when two parties come to meet they will often sit on opposite sides of a table. This is automatically adversarial in terms of the territory. There is now a "my side" and a "your side," with a large gulf in between. It is easy, then, for *groups* to sit on either side of a table and unwittingly set up an adversarial meeting of "your team against my team." For example, parliaments are often deliberately set up in this aggressive manner, with the psychological barrier of a no-man's-land that people are traditionally banned from crossing (unless they are changing their allegiance, or "crossing the floor," as it is called). In order to overcome this problem in a business setting, you can simply mix up potentially adversarial groups with each other. Doing so quickly breaks down the power of the largest antagonistic marker in the space (the table) and discourages "taking sides." You will be helping people to see others' points of view by placing them where they can literally get the best perspective.

Playing to a Crowd

Remember, once a person sees more than four people at one time, her unconscious mind defines that number as *lots*, or *a crowd*. How intimidating it is, then, for someone to walk into a room with anything more than four people in it: "Oh, no, a gang!"

Figure 11.2 Gang of Five

The solution to this problem is that if you wish to create an environment that is welcoming to potential clients or partners, you should organize your team in such a way that you break up the numbers of people grouped together so that your team is less intimidating when guests enter a meeting room. If you wish to be most inviting to a business guest or group entering a space, be sure that the people who are receiving the guests are grouped in twos or threes, rather than standing around looking like a big gang (Figure 11.2).

Distance Learning

The details of the ways we treat territory and a group (or groups) within it are mapped out in the work of anthropologist Edward Hall, who had a great rule that described his theory on the effect of people being close or far away from each other, or *proxemics*, as it became known: "Like gravity, the influence of two bodies on each other is inversely proportional not only to the square of their distance but possibly even the cube of the distance between them." So, the closer you come to someone, the greater your influence over him becomes, and, of course, the greater his influence over you.

Body spacing and posture, according to Hall, are unconscious reactions to often subtle changes in nonverbal communication. Social distance between people, he believed, could be reliably correlated with physical distance, i.e., people of equal status will be physically closer than those of unequal status just as the closer you are to someone emotionally, the closer you become physically, all of this according to the following delineations made by Hall in his *American Anthropologist* article "A System for the Notation of Proxemic Behavior":

- *Intimate distance*, used for embracing, touching, or whispering: close phase, less than 6 inches (15 cm); far phase, 6 to 18 inches (15 to 45 cm).
- *Personal distance*, used for interactions among good friends: close phase, 1.5 to 2.5 feet (45 to 75 cm); far phase, 2.5 to 4 feet (75 to 120 cm).
- *Social distance*, used for interactions among acquaintances: close phase, 4 to 7 feet (1.2 to 2.1 m); far phase, 7 to 12 feet (2.1 to 3.6 m).
- *Public distance*, used for public speaking: close phase, 12 to 25 feet (3.6 to 7.5 m); far phase, 25 feet (7.5 m) or more.

From these guidelines, you can see that as a presenter or speaker, the further you are away from your audience, the less social, personal, or intimate effect you are able to have upon them. Therefore, we might say that in order to create more impact on the members of your audience, you must have greater spatial intimacy with them, and so one would guess that you should move toward them (and there are many communication coaches who say exactly that).

However, we must bear in mind how easy it is to cross important boundaries of spatial acceptability (as we have been looking at with respect to status infringement through accidentally laying claim to another person's territory by "getting in his space"). It is simply not enough to say that "trust increases when we move closer to people" or that you should "move into the personal space of the audience to make key points in your presentation more impactful." You also run the risk of intimidating your listeners and lowering their status with this same move, either through towering over them from on top of a stage, or looming over them seated (as though you have the "higher ground," so to speak), or by invading their space by getting too close. The latter is easily counteracted by using the following principle: When you are communicating live and in close proximity, if you move into a position that is so close that you cannot see the feet of others while making eye contact, it is likely that they cannot see yours. Once they cannot see your feet, you have crossed an important *spatial boundary*, because they will not be able to predict your gross body movement without dropping their eye contact from your face, where they are trying to judge the finer elements of "feeling." From a distance at which your audience members can see your whole body, they are able to predict both intention and feeling. In physical performance this is know as "the throw." Go beyond the throw and you intimidate and initiate a retreat or attack response.

So if you cannot see each other's feet in your lower peripheral vision, some kind of physical contact (often a handshake) will be necessary in the business context to positively establish trust.

How High?

How does our physical height factor into all this? Historically, raising or lowering your "height" in relation to another person has been used as a means of establishing either a superior or a subordinate relationship; in other words, raising or lower your *status* in relation to another. We refer to a member of royalty as "Your Highness," whereas individuals who commit negative acts are called "low," "low-down," or "lowlife." Who among us wants to be "looked down on," or to "fall short" of the targets? And equally so none of us wants to be perceived as being on our "high horse," "on a pedestal," or all "high and mighty."

An expert business body language practitioner should regard his physical height only as a tool to help others, not to dominate others. If you are taller than most, whether you are male or female, your body will look naturally dominant (especially if you are also broad across your shoulders—true for both men and women). Vertically blessed readers of this book, you come to the table with high status already programmed into your appearance! If you then start to add further signals of dominance—a loud voice; bigger and broader gestures; clothing colored with aggressive reds or black and yellow combinations (used in nature as warning signals, no less)—then you stand an excellent chance of unwittingly being very threatening to others at a base brain level. For those of you who are shorter than the average, give yourself a little more distance from those who are taller than you. Your slightly more distant perspective of taller people will make them appear less vertically dominating to you and stop you from having to hold your head at a full 90-degree angle to make eye contact.

Too often however, extremely tall people unconsciously compensate for their natural status edge by stooping over and lowering their heads so as not to dominate their shorter superiors in the organization. Again, the solution for the tall is quite similar to that for the short: simply step back a bit and you will automatically become less dominant, without having to try to lower your physical presence by stooping and crunching in at the stomach, collapsing the chest, and putting yourself on a negative out breath.

Live Long and Prosper

Despite what we may wish to believe, many height studies show that on the whole, taller people are more successful, are healthier, and live longer than short people. For example, a 2006 *New York Times* article cites a group of epidemiologists at the University of Bristol in England who have published studies showing that taller people, after controlling for various factors, are less likely to die of coronary heart disease, respiratory disease, and stomach cancer than shorter people. The underlying socio-economic foundation for this may be in a study from one institute of management that recorded the heights and salaries of well over 2,000 managers at the director level and found that every inch of height above the company norm added almost $1,000 to that person's salary package, and this held true equally for both sexes. Other studies have also shown that height is linked to financial success: in one study focusing on Wall Street, every inch of height added $600 to a person's bottom line. The same correlation has also been found in government departments and universities, where people are supposedly promoted based on their competence, not their height. One American study showed that tall people not only got the best jobs in American firms, but also received higher starting salaries. Those who were over 6 feet 2 inches tall got 12 percent more than those who were less than 6 feet!

Short of your taking this information and immediately buying platform heels or booking a major operation to extend your legs, the business body language technique that will help you is to simply *stand tall*; if you are already tall in stature, you should still stand tall, but be aware that if you are physically dominating others, this can cause the fight-or-flight response. Remember, successful executive managers use the skills of influence and persuasion that we have outlined in previous chapters to mitigate the potential threat that their height might bring. Humans are looking for a strong person who will be on our side—not one who will be against us. Do not heed the advice of Machiavelli to the Prince: "It is better to be feared than loved." He died in poverty 13 years after writing his famous treatise on government. Clearly he had no trusted friends by then, and he probably was not feared by too many people at that point either, at least not in any advantageous kind of way.

And for the majority of us who are not the tallest people in the room—don't worry! You can still command status at any height. Research has found that the more someone is perceived as having high status in an organization, the more he is also perceived as being taller than he really is. Indeed, in one university experiment, a student talking to other students who had been introduced as *their professor* was perceived as being half a foot taller than when she was introduced to a different group of students as their peer. No wonder a simple promotion in title can sometimes be more effective in retaining key people than a raise in salary. A greater amount on your personal pay-slip does not make you appear to be taller and more powerful to anyone, yet a company news letter congratulating you on your move up from vice president to senior vice president could potentially give you a three-inch height advantage in terms of perception. And perception is reality. Fake it and you'll make it!

But what of the integrity of your authenticity, you might ask? Well, I say that it is only *the experience* that others have of you and that you have of yourself that can be considered genuine. So use your imagination and enjoy creating a great experience around yourself and allow your audience to feel what is authentic about it. As the famous American writer William S. Burroughs said, "You cannot fake quality any more than you can fake a good meal." And after all, the Scarecrow in *The Wizard of Oz* needed only to receive the physical diploma, not the actual education, to recognize that he had an extraordinary brain.

Perspective Makes a Difference

It is easy to change physical position or perspective and, by doing so, change the brain's perception and functioning. Try this on for size: sit in a chair and get someone to stand close and over you to maximize the height difference. Next, ask this person to reprimand you as loudly and forcefully as possible. Then change positions: you stand up while your colleague sits and reprimands you from the chair. You'll find that not only will your colleague find it nearly impossible to do this, but his voice will sound different and lack any authority. Of course, this is unusual (and could look kind of silly at the office), but it will give you a sense of how well you listened to your reprimand and the attitude it produced in you when you were being height-dominated. Did you notice your fight-or-flight mechanism kicking in? Try repeating the same exercise with your colleague at different levels of sitting, standing, and even lying down. When someone is lying down, the difference will be far more pronounced—you won't take the reprimand seriously at all.

Breaking Down the Barriers to Communication

Whether you are communicating with one person in a room or with many people in a meeting, the fewer barriers there are between you and your audience, the better for persuasion and influence. Here are some further ideas for controlling the space to your advantage.

In rooms, you could take away the table between people, or at least to communicate nonverbally over the top of the table as much as possible. You could also seat yourself at the corner of the table at a 90° angle to the other party in order to minimize the barrier and the "you versus me" message of 180° positioning, but still leave some element of table space between you so that the other party can feel safe.

When you are standing up to present, you need to balance the height advantage against the height dominance. The fact that those sitting close to you now have your hands at their eye level can be really quite threatening. They simply will not be able to listen if your hands are intimidating them at this unconscious level. It is often prudent to put yourself a few people away from any key decision makers; by having a safe barrier between their seated positions and you standing, they will feel protected and more relaxed. Also, you can think about placing them to your left. Doing so can cause the image of these powerful people to be processed in the more creative part of your mind; thus, you will be able to interpret consciously any of their body language as having more opportunity—being more positive. When you see them in this way, you are more likely to give positive body language, and they are more likely to mirror this back at you. When they are placed on your right, you are more predisposed to think of them as critical and look at them with a frown, and so, in turn, they will mirror this back at you. Or even worse, you will ignore them altogether, and they may well ignore you.

It is really quite interesting how *where* an individual member of an audience places herself in the group has an effect on the information that she takes away with her. With this in mind, it is useful to explore how you can orchestrate who sits where, depending on the strategy you have for whom you need to influence and, conversely, who really does not matter so much. Of course, it would be lovely if the world conformed to the idea that everyone is equally important, but that is just not true, now, is it? Not all members of a business audience have equal power. And so, to optimize your effectiveness and efficiency in meeting your objectives, you must focus on the influencers and the decision makers.

Noted body language writers Allan and Barbara Pease conducted an interesting study in which they observed the manner and extent to which delegates participated in a seminar based on where they were sitting in the room, and also how much of the presenter's content they could recall afterward. The result was what the Peases called the *funnel effect*. When the participants were sitting in a "classroom style," there appeared to be a "learning zone," shaped like a funnel, that extended directly down the center of the audience and across the front row. Those sitting in the open end of the "funnel" participated the most, interacted most with the presenter, and most recalled the content after the event. Those who participated least were those sitting in the back or to the sides; this group tended to be more negative about the seminar, was more confrontational, and had the lowest recall.

An Experiment in Learning

We might expect that the people who are most enthusiastic about learning about the topic would be the ones who would choose to sit closest to the front, and those who are least enthusiastic would sit in the back or to the sides. With this assumption, the Peases conducted a further experiment to determine whether the funnel effect was a result of where people *chose* to sit based on their interest in the topic, and also whether where a person sat affected his level of participation and retention of content *regardless of interest.*

They found that regardless of the prelearning level of interest, participants who were placed up front retained more information after the event and participated more; the participants who were placed to the back and sides retained less than usual and participated less. If you want someone to really get the message, then orchestrate the seating arrangement so that key decision makers or thought leaders are placed up front or in the funnel. Or follow in the footsteps of some presenters and trainers by abandoning the classroom-style meeting concept for speaking to or training smaller groups, and replace it with the horseshoe. Evidence suggests that horseshoe seating results in more participation and better recall as a result of the increased eye contact between all attendees and the speaker. Of course, sometimes you have little control over the setting for your communication, but when you do, you can now use that ability to orchestrate the seating arrangement in order to orchestrate the outcomes.

Engaging with Your Team

Your body language in groups is important when you are presenting as part of a team. The audience will be watching the body language of not just whoever is presenting at any given moment, but also the other members of that team who are not speaking. How the nonspeaking members are poised indicates to the onlooker how well regarded each team member is within the team—and is therefore an indicator of team unity. A united team equals a strong team equals a strong offering of a product or service. When you are presenting with your team, the simplest and most effective way to get the message that your team is strong across to your audience nonverbally is that whenever one member of the team is speaking, everyone else thinks to themselves, "My friend who is speaking right now is amazing." The audience will notice the subtle body language that this mantra produces and will tend to mirror it. How simple it is to influence and persuade an audience into joining with a feeling. Equally so, how easy it is to pay *no* attention to how you reflect upon others with your nonverbal communication, and bring the whole team and project down as a result. Of course, not only can you stir feelings within your audience, but you can also take your audience on *a journey* of feeling—and this is what we will look at in the final chapter.

Chapter 11 Quick Study

Despite the suits and ties, businesspeople are territorial animals. You must be respectful of that territory or you will cause them to retreat or advance aggressively with respect to you and your ideas.

Just Do This Now

1. To gain trust whenever you approach another person, display open gestures and show the palms of your hands in the TruthPlane.

2. Once you are within the distance where you cannot see the feet of whomever you are talking with in your peripheral vision while maintaining eye contact, extend your hand and give that person an upper-hand handshake with a light smile to put him at ease.

3. To build good rapport, find ways to sit or stand that do not put large barriers between you and others, block exits, or cause you to overshadow others with your height.

Chapter 11 Case Study

Theory to Practice: Networking

You are at a networking cocktail evening, and suddenly you are at "alert." The woman across the room is the very person who can best help take your career to the next level, and here is your chance to make an impression and hopefully secure a follow-up meeting. The stakes are high, and you want to make sure you do everything right. Silently, you ponder how your approach should change in different cases. What should you do if she is

- Standing up across the room?
- There when you turn around?
- Sitting at a table or on a couch?

Insight 1: Standing Up across the Room

If you are approaching someone new from a distance, ensure that he can see all of you as soon as possible. If you can't see someone's feet, your defensive reactions are initiated. It may be a matter of determining your timing so that the target person has a complete view of you as you approach.

Insight 2: There When You Turn Around

In some networking environments (often the more popular ones), cramped quarters can limit your ability to provide your "full view." Also, serendipity may put a target person around a corner or in at the back of you as you turn. If this is the case, you can counter the natural territorial defenses by making body contact through a handshake. Quickly sending a message of safety will increase the effectiveness of a first interaction.

Insight 3: Sitting at a Table or on a Couch

Recalling the imperative of status, it is important that you get to the other person's "level" as soon as possible in the interaction. Taking a seat, squatting, and down on one knee are effective ways to reduce height differentials. Everyone is familiar with the discomfort of having someone hover around your table or, worse, behind or beside your office chair.

Provocation

How is someone invading your territory? How are you mirroring this behaviour and invading his in return, or invading others that are less protected'?

Moving Your Audience

Strategies for Nonverbal Influence

It is not the strongest of the species nor the most intelligent that survives. It is the one that is the most adaptable to change.
—Charles Darwin

In this chapter you'll learn:

- What a "physical narrative" is
- How Hollywood can help you make your case
- The Fact, Care, Do structure
- How to move your audience emotionally on *any* subject
- How to use the "Zeigarnik effect" to keep your audience hooked

If you reflect on all the persuasive nonverbal techniques that are now in your possession, you may notice that a great deal of emphasis has been placed on the benefits of making very clear choices and sticking to them. Hopefully, you will have even adopted the mantra, "Make a choice, make it bigger, keep it tidy." In this final chapter, you are going to learn how to apply this idea in different contexts and with a few twists to engage an audience with your message even further. We are going to investigate how to further maximize your influence by actually *moving the audience*, provoking its members to journey through certain emotional and intellectual states when we speak. We will also look at *physical change* as a way to influence—a clear departure from some of the previous techniques, which focused on physical stability and constancy as a tool.

In other words, now that we understand the rules, we can understand how to break them effectively. If you have been practicing the techniques throughout this book and are beginning to master nonverbal communication in business—getting closer and closer to presenting at your best every time—you are ready for this next step. Even if you have mastered the fundamentals, it's important that you leave room for variation. Great leaders such as JFK have said, "Change is the law of life and without attention to it we miss the future." For your own progress with the important work of this book, you must recognize, as the first century BC proverb writer Publilius Syrus did, that "It's a bad plan that admits no modification." And it is this effective use of change and surprise that we will look at right now.

Physical Narrative

At the heart of any communication tactic, and at the core of any strategic approach to getting a message across, exists a necessary skill. Anyone who wants to build trust in business simply must have the capacity and to *influ-*

ence human decision making—to be a great *persuader.* Such a person must have the ability to modify the actions of others in accordance with his own desires. As modern depth psychology has shown, the human unconscious mind expresses itself in images, metaphors and symbols rather than in words of concrete meaning. If you wish to have a conversation with your own and your audience's unconscious master, in order to influence it at the deepest levels, you must do the same. With *nonverbal* influence and persuasion techniques, you are physically, vocally and environmentally expressing images, metaphors and symbols that can quickly move people through a progression of deep changes—whether it be toward a new feeling, a new thought, or a new physical place.

Not by coincidence, the idea of moving an audience through a progression of changes is also the function of a story or a narrative. Without change, there is no story. So in order to take an audience on a journey to a new feeling or thought, and furthermore, to persuade its members to make decisions that are in line with *your* own goals, you have to take them through some changes in their own physicality. Let's investigate further.

Hollywood

Just take a look at the classic structure of a Hollywood film, a perfect example of the modern version of storytelling. Syd Field, one of the most popular screenwriting gurus of recent years in the film industry, has written several books on the subject of story structure. His ideas about what makes a good script have become very influential. In his articulation of the ideal "three-act structure," he describes how a film must begin with "setup" information (Act One); only after this can the protagonist experience the "inciting incident" that gives her a goal, which must then be achieved. The protagonist's struggle is to achieve this goal, the "confrontation" (Act Two), is a more subtle turning point with an often devastating reversal of the protagonist's fortunes. The final element (Act Three) of the film depicts a climactic struggle by the protagonist to finally achieve her goal and the aftermath of this struggle.

Certainly, it is very fair to say that the majority of the classic story structure is built around the protagonist's encountering a problem and then solving it. It is with this in mind that your nonverbal communication must be adaptable, able to move your audience beyond the impasse and to transform it and others in the process. So let's look at exactly how to use *nonverbal progression* to move through a simple story and create quite an impact on your audience.

The Setup Let's look at a business message that you are delivering to a group that, although its members are already working well together, needs further motivation to keep doing well—to stay ahead of the game.

First, we need to understand that if the group is already doing well, then its members may not be actively looking for new or further opportunities. So the story, "You are doing great. . . . Now how about we work harder and do even better!" probably will not motivate the audience.

To put it in terms of Syd Field, the setup of the story is, "Things are going great." To move things along further, you might drop in this comment, which acts as the inciting incident: "But when we look over our shoulders, we can see the competition, not only coming to take away the extra resources that we have accumulated, but threatening the very foundations upon which all of this is built!" This story structure is compelling because it swiftly takes the audience from pleasure to pain—in essence, the common Hollywood dramatic model.

We needed words to help us deliver the inciting incident, but it takes rock-solid body language skills to get the message across fully and inspire the audience to react appropriately. Before we progress to looking at how to move the audience back toward pleasure, let's see how, using our non-verbal communication skill, we *physically* move our listeners from pleasure to pain along with this verbal narrative.

Acts of Transformation

One of my most influential mentors was once giving a speech in the streets and, being quite the agent provocateur, was managing to whip the assembled crowd into a very aggressive fervor—not *for* him, but *against* him. He riled up the crowd to such an extent that they chased him across the city with a mind to beat another point of view into him. A master of transformation, he ducked into an alley as the crowd passed and tagged onto the end of the mob—screaming for his own death! Studying with him, I understood that adaptability is the only surefire strategy for success (and survival), and I work with all my clients to help them have a high degree of that adaptability when they communicate so that they can *accept* the most extreme and often dangerous situations—working with them rather than against them.

The Confrontation The first part of this presentation or speech—we'll call it "You're Great!"—can be performed starting in the TruthPlane because you are stating a fact: it is *great* that the team is great at what it does, and its members should rightly be praised. They trust this message that they see in the TruthPlane, and they will continue to listen because they are gaining status and their brain's reward system will be delivering pleasure to them. You can choose to increase the level of excitement in this first part of your speech—raise their heart rate, breathing, and blood pressure—by bringing your gestures up into the PassionPlane when you are describing the team's achievements and how it has exceeded expectations by delivering above and beyond what others might normally have achieved (because you started your speech in the TruthPlane, this will seem like a natural progression, rather than an exaggeration).

Moving into the PassionPlane at this stage is particularly advantageous in the context of applying our Hollywood story structure to this communication: raising the energy and passion just before the drop that is about to come will maximize the effect—both physically and emotionally—of the inciting incident. Your audience is receiving its reward, and your increased excitement is adding further positive stimulation to the reward processes in the brain. Now, just as those in your audience are getting hooked on the increased levels of their own dopamine, you are going to drop a bombshell and send them into withdrawal, both physically and mentally.

The Climactic Struggle Now you have entered the final part of the three-act structure. Drop your actions back down to the TruthPlane, and let the audience know that there is a problem. Now, people don't generally like problems when they are confronted with them directly; they can switch off mentally from them as an avoidance of the threat, or even mentally downplay their own involvement in the problem (sidestepping the issue or passing the buck.) To avoid this outcome, we'll use a device based on the Zeigarnik effect. Bluma Zeigarnik was a Russian psychologist who, in the 1920s, discovered the principle that explains that an unfinished idea sticks in the mind better than a finished one (more on this suspense technique later). Zeigarnik's principle basically means that you can keep an audience hooked by saying, "There is a solution, which I will talk about once you understand just how severe the problem is." At this point, you drop your arms to the GrotesquePlane. Now you can go into the negative details.

Since you have been in the TruthPlane prior to this, confirming facts that the audience knows to be true, you will have established trust. The audience members will now emotionally follow your drop into the GrotesquePlane and be likely to take your bad news seriously. They can hear the tone of your voice and see your body. They can see the physical change that this story is making in you, and they begin to copy it. The change is stark enough to cause them to be withdrawn from their pleasurable state. They now demand the restoration of the good feeling that they had been in previously. They want you (and, by extension, themselves) to get back up to truth and passion—and away from the grotesque.

When you next *lay down the solution* for them, moving back into the TruthPlane, they immediately follow, willingly joining in with this new feeling and buying into the solution you propose. You can once again take them with you back toward and into passion as you describe the great results that they will have once again from their now-renewed extra effort.

Persuasive

In following this structure, you are using nonverbal communication to cause an audience to motivate itself: you are producing a compelling physiological imperative that assigns greater meaning to the less tangible business imperative. In other words, the potential pain of losing business opportunities is not as tangible as the current discomfort caused by the withdrawal of pleasurable chemicals in the brain that your nonverbal messages are instigating. By overlapping these nonverbal cues with your verbal content, you have effectively attached the feeling of pain to the business prognosis—and now the potential for pain makes sense because it *feels* real, and feeling is reality because it is the meaning that we attach to whatever we sense.

You are now using body language to create emotional meaning around the words and linguistic images that you are creating.

Body Language Is Real Language

Just as in any communication system, the more versed you become in the meaning of the vocabulary you use, the more power you have over yourself and therefore over others. Notice that in the example given, the manipulative effect is very powerful and clear. Yes, we are talking about being manipulative, and that's because *all* use of language is manipulative. Language is a tool that can be used for good, bad, and everything in between. The choice of how to use that tool is yours. Indeed, it stands to reason that much of the time we are accidentally and unconsciously manipulating others with our tools of language.

Your aim in reading this book should be to understand how to use the tool of nonverbal communication to consciously manipulate your audience, for good or bad (preferably good), but never, never by accident. As Dr. Frank Lutz, the renowned Republican pollster and linguistic engineer of consent during the Bush administration, says, "It's not what you say, it's what people hear."

You have the opportunity to become an artist—a poet with your *nonverbal communication*, and affect those around you purposefully, elegantly, and with the potential for great returns. However, this work is only for the brave and the bold. Remember the words of British author George Orwell, whose intense opposition to totalitarianism and passion for clarity in language led him to say, "During times of universal deceit, telling the truth becomes a revolutionary act."

Verse and Chapter

So let's now create a really short nonverbal progression and some linguistics to go with it to illustrate how simple and poetic the proper usage can be. You are going to move from the TruthPlane to the PassionPlane and then back to the TruthPlane again. This is a very simple *rule of three* narrative progression that comes full circle in terms of the physical positions taken. The rule of three narrative model is very important to nonverbal communication, as it has a natural suspension programmed into it. For example, One and Two set up the expectation of Three, which can either fulfill the expectation or surprise the audience.

In Japanese Noh theater, there is a traditional narrative progression in three parts called the *jo*, the *ha*, and the *kyu*. This is a form of telling stories that was hit upon by Zeami (a Japanese classical dramatic writer of the thirteenth century). *Jo-ha-kyu* means anticipation, release, payoff. Tension builds, bursts into climax, and finishes quickly. All of this has similarities to the Western concept (Aristotle's) of thesis, antithesis, synthesis.

Okay, so clearly the rule of three story structure is classic. Now let's add physicality to a textual structure that I call Fact, Care, Do. First off, during the anticipation created in the TruthPlane, you tell the audience a "Fact." This should usually encompass some problem facing your audience; because the problem is unresolved at this point, the audience members experience anticipation, or suspension, that will keep them "hooked" as they journey with you through the next two parts. Also, because the problem is delivered in the TruthPlane and with the YesState, they are engaged by it, not driven away by it. And, of course, the *fact* of the problem is sincerely expressed in the TruthPlane and accepted as truthful by the audience.

Next, we move to the "Care" element of the piece. This part consists of you describing the emotional bond with the problem: how you and your audience care about the problem and the feelings it provokes. Remember, people buy into the *feeling*, not the text. Your hands should be lifted into the PassionPlane at this point in order to escalate people's heart rates and breathing intensity at this moment.

During this part of the Fact, Care, Do sequence, you are raising the level of suspense—there is as yet no resolution, either physically or in the content. Your audience members are hooked in with the suspense, both in their bodies and in their minds. Both the *fact* and the *care* are part of the anticipation segment of this story structure—so, now comes the release that will move your listeners toward the payoff.

You lower your hands to the TruthPlane once again, and there is now a sense of completion to the movement and an imposed sigh of relief as you explain what you/they are going to *do* about this problem, and how much you care about it. Your listeners are now attaching the feeling of relief to the *action* that you are talking about. Only now are they predisposed to accept and agree with the course of action that you describe, because they can literally *feel* how it brings them back to a more stable, pleasurable state, away from the suspense and anxiety over the subject. The payoff for all this is the action that they will now *do* for you to keep this state stable. Often you can linguistically state the action that you are looking for in the "Do" part of the structure.

It's quite a simple plan programmed with archetypal resonance: movement that can connect directly with your audiences' deepest decision making faculty—the unconscious. Your mental intention behind the message has been solidified within a concrete action plan. Now you can mentally relax and allow yourself to be adaptable to playing your audience with these movements. You can be open to them, available to their reactions. You now have the golden opportunity of truly moving out together on your vision.

Language and Power

All that remains now is for you to personally explore the vocabulary of physical language that you are now able to bring to your messages. Practice the simplicity of this language and see for yourself how, by employing it, you can directly affect your audience. Be careful never to get stuck in a rut of nonverbal norms: your power to survive is in your power to adapt. Adaptation is the gift that keeps all life on earth thriving in an environment that changes by the minute.

Don't get stale in your physicality—keep moving and keep changing, and you will be able to cross from business niche to business niche with great fluidity and elegance. Your communication ability is founded on not only your desire to change the opinions of others, but your openness to changing your own opinion as well. The information in this book will give you the most solid foundation for your own personal exploration, and final mastery, of how you nonverbally communicate with those around you for business persuasion and influence. So I urge you now to immediately use anything that is working for you, and recommend that you immediately discard anything that is not. Using *focus* and *simplicity* to discard is more powerful than "practice makes perfect" for methods that do not instantly resonate with you.

Now that you possess the fundamentals, it's time to let your own experimentation with and testing of techniques inspire new ideas. Quickly you'll discover which techniques work best toward your goal of artful and effective communication. As you expand your knowledge and experience with these nonverbal techniques and become increasingly savvy at using your body language, you will hone your own personal style in the art of nonverbal communication.

Thank you for reading this book. I hope that the words I have written have led you to an understanding of some new and advanced techniques in nonverbal influence and persuasion, and also an understanding of the bigger communication picture and what that means to us all. I would like to leave you with one irrefutable idea, an idea that is as fundamental to nonverbal communication as it is to verbal. Keep this quote in mind as you journey forward with persuasion and influence through your mastery in business of winning body language:

> *Broadly speaking, the short words are the best, and*
> *the old words best of all.*
> —Winston Churchill

Chapter 12 Quick Study

Attaching gestures that create feeling to narrative structure compels an audience through a progression of feeling; an audience can be influenced to feel an emotional connection with information that would otherwise have had little effect on it. Therefore, you can get an audience emotionally involved in just about anything by attaching the right progression of nonverbal communication.

Just Do This Now

1. Use Fact, Care, Do to give a simple three-part story structure in your presentation.

2. Attach clear nonverbal gestures to a compelling narrative in order to move your audience toward an emotional state in response to your presentation. For example, give a fact in the TruthPlane, explain how the audience might care about that fact in the PassionPlane, and then explain what you are all going to do about it back in the TruthPlane.

3. Take the audience members on a clear physical journey that will persuade them to act upon your advice.

Chapter 12 Case Study

Theory to Practice: Drama and Business, a Winning Combination

Jay has developed a start-up company into a successful and sustainable business. The growth numbers have been impressive: from three employees six years ago to approaching one hundred this past quarter. However, Jay is worried that the necessary formalization of some business processes has reduced the level of passion in the organization. He used to be directly involved in all hires, but there are a number of employees with whom he has had little meaningful interaction, if he has had any at all.

He is addressing an all-hands meeting later this month, and he wants to send a number of messages. The business is solid and sustainable, but he also wants to counter any feelings of complacency because the company isn't doubling its revenues anymore. Last year's revenue growth was a mere 4 percent.

Insight

Employees and others who are involved in the success of an organization deserve to be told a story that involves feeling and emotion. They are entitled to some drama. A speaker who is comfortable using different techniques can orchestrate her body language to fit with the structure of her speech in telling the story.

One effective structure is Fact, Care, Do. In the example given here, the Fact portion of the discussion could focus on the negatives of revenue growth, in comparative terms, changing from "triple-digit" to merely a "single digit." The body language here could veer into the out breath and GrotesquePlane areas with demonstrably less energy and tension. This can contrast with moving into the Care area, where TruthPlane language instills safety and trust in the things that are going well, and the company remains solid. Do, which speaks to actions moving forward, can be punctuated with PassionPlane gestures and elevated levels of tension and involvement.

As with any story or drama, the telling is as important as the scripting.

Provocation

With all that you understand now of winning body language, how will the story change for you and where do you see it ending?

Concluding Thought

Intelligence is the capacity to receive, decode and transmit information efficiently. Stupidity is blockage of this process at any point.

—Robert Anton Wilson

(January 18, 1932–January 11, 2007)

Appendix

The GesturePlane System

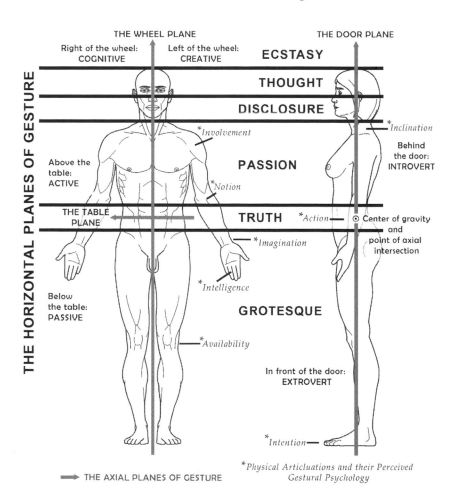

THE WHEEL PLANE

Right of the wheel: COGNITIVE Left of the wheel: CREATIVE

THE DOOR PLANE

ECSTASY

THOUGHT

DISCLOSURE

*Involvement

*Inclination

Behind the door: INTROVERT

Above the table: ACTIVE

PASSION

*Notion

THE HORIZONTAL PLANES OF GESTURE

THE TABLE PLANE

TRUTH

*Action

⊙ Center of gravity and point of axial intersection

*Imagination

Below the table: PASSIVE

*Intelligence

GROTESQUE

*Availability

In front of the door: EXTROVERT

*Intention

THE AXIAL PLANES OF GESTURE

*Physical Articulations and their Perceived Gestural Psychology

Further Reading and Resources

A list of books and articles referred to, consulted, or of related interest:

Alexander, F. Matthias, and Edward Maisel. *The Alexander Technique*. London: Thames and Hudson, 1974.

Amighi, Janet Kestenberg. *The Meaning of Movement: Developmental and Clinical Perspectives of the Kestenberg Movement Profile*. New York: Routledge, 1999.

Ardrey, Robert, and Berdine Ardrey. *The Territorial Imperative: A Personal Inquiry into the Animal Origins of Property and Nations*. New York: Atheneum, 1966.

Ariely, Dan. *Predictably Irrational: The Hidden Forces That Shape Our Decisions*. New York: HarperCollins, 2008.

Atkinson, Anthony. "Impaired Recognition of Emotions from Body Movements Is Associated with Elevated Motion Coherence Thresholds in Autism Spectrum Disorders." *Neuropsychologia* 47(13), 2009.

Bandler, Richard, and John Grinder. *The Structure of Magic*. 2 vols. Palo Alto, Calif.: Science and Behavior Books, 1976.

Bandler, Richard, and John La Valle. *Persuasion Engineering*. Capitola, Calif.: Meta Publications, 1996.

Barba, Eugenio, and Nicola Savarese. *A Dictionary of Theatre Anthropology: The Secret Art of the Performer*. London: Routledge, 1991.

Bates, Brian. *The Way of the Actor: A Path to Knowledge and Power*. Boston: Shambhala, 1987

Campbell, Alastair. *The Blair Years: Extracts from the Alastair Campbell Diaries*. New York: Knopf, 2007.

Carnegie, Dale. *How to Win Friends and Influence People*. New York: Simon & Schuster, 1934.

Chekhov, Michael. *To the Actor: On the Technique of Acting*. New York: HarperCollins, 1993.

Cialdini, Robert. *Influence: Science and Practice*. Pearson, 2009

Darwin, Charles. *Works of Charles Darwin: including* On the Origin of Species, The Descent of Man, The Expression of Emotions in Man and Animals. MobileReference Kindle Edition, 2000.

Dawkins, Richard. *The Selfish Gene*. Oxford, U.K.: Oxford University Press, 1989.

Ekman, Paul. *What the Face Reveals*. New York: Oxford University Press, 1997.

Erickson, Milton H. *Hypnotic Realities*. New York: Irvington Publishers, 1976.

Feldenkrais, Moshé. *Awareness through Movement*. New York: Harper & Row, 1972.

Hall, Edward T. "A System for the Notation of Proxemic Behaviour." *American Anthropologist* 65, 1963.

Howard, Eliot. *Territory in Bird Life*. Atheneum, 1964.

James, William. *The Meaning of Truth*. New York: Longmans, 1909.

Johnstone, Keith. *Impro: Improvisation and the Theatre*. New York: Theatre Arts Book, 1987.

Kohler, Evelyne. "Hearing Sounds, Understanding Actions: Action Representation in Mirror Neurons." *Science* 297, 2002.

Kruger, Justin, and David Dunning. "Unskilled and Unaware of It: How Difficulties in Recognizing One's Own Incompetence Lead to Inflated Self-Assessments." *Journal of Personality and Social Psychology* 77(6), 1999

Lakoff, George, and Mark Johnson. *Philosophy in the Flesh: The Embodied Mind and Its Challenge to Western Thought.* New York: Basic Books, 1999.

Lecoq, Jacques. *The Moving Body: Teaching Creative Theatre.* New York: Routledge, 2001.

Lecoq, Jacques, and David Bradby. *Theatre of Movement and Gesture.* London: Routledge, 2006.

Lindstrom, Martin. *Buyology: Truth and Lies about Why We Buy.* New York: Doubleday, 2008.

Lopata, Andy, and Peter Roper. . . . *And Death Came Third!* Lean Marketing Press, 2006.

Luntz, Frank. *Words That Work: It's Not What You Say, It's What People Hear.* New York: Hyperion, 2007.

Maeda, John. *The Laws of Simplicity.* Cambridge, Mass.: MIT Press, 2006.

Mamet, David. *True and False: Heresy and Common Sense for the Actor.* New York: Pantheon, 1997.

Marmot, Michael. *The Status Syndrome: How Social Standing Affects Our Health and Longevity.* New York: Henry Holt, 2005.

Mehrabian, Albert, and Susan R. Ferris. "Inference of Attitudes from Nonverbal Communication in Two Channels." *Journal of Consulting Psychology* 31(3), 1967.

Mehrabian, Albert, and Morton Wiener. "Decoding of Inconsistent Communications." *Journal of Personality and Social Psychology* 6(1), 1967.

Mirodan, Vladimir. "The Way of Transformation: the Laban-Malmgren System of Dramatic Character Analysis." University of London, 1997.

Palmer, Wendy. *The Intuitive Body: Discovering the Wisdom of Conscious Embodiment and Aikido.* Blue Snake Books, 2008.

Pease, Allan, and Barbara Pease. *The Definitive Book of Body Language.* New York: Bantam, 2006.

Crowley, Aleister. *The Book of Lies.* London: Weiland & Co., 1913.

Ramachandran, V. S. *A Brief Tour of Human Consciousness: From Impostor Poodles to Purple Numbers.* New York: Pi Press, 2005.

Ramachakara, Yogi. *Science of Breath.* London: L. N. Fowler & Co Ltd., 1960.

Renvoisé, Patrick, and Christopher Morin. *Neuromarketing: Selling to the Old Brain.* Nashville, Tenn.: T. Nelson, 2007

Rock, David. "SCARF: A Brain-Based Model for Collaborating with and Influencing Others." *NeuroLeadership Journal* 1, 2008.

Shaw, Bernard. *Voice-Overs: A Practical Guide.* New York: Routledge, 2000.

Sperry, Roger Wolcott, and Paul A. Sperry. *Science and Moral Priority: Merging Mind, Brain, and Human Values.* New York: Columbia University Press, 1990

Strozzi-Heckler, Richard. *The Leadership Dojo: Build Your Foundation as an Exemplary Leader.* Frog Books, 2007

Thouless, Robert H. *Straight and Crooked Thinking.* Hodder Arnold H & S, 1990.

Waysun Liao. *T'ai Chi Classics.* Boston: Shambhala, 2000.

Wright, John. *Why Is That So Funny? A Practical Exploration of Physical Comedy.* London: Nick Hern Books, 2006.

Zeami and William Scott Wilson. *The Flowering Spirit: Classic Teachings on the Art of Noh.* Tokyo: Kodansha, 2006.

Index

Note: Boldface numbers indicate
illustrations.

Message in communication, 2

Method acting, 46. *See also* Theater and body language

Microexpressions/microgestures, facial expression and, 97

Mimes and communication, 11, 28–29, 132

Mind, unconscious. *See* Unconscious mind

Mirror neuron system, 132

Mixed messages/signals, 27
facial expressions and, 98, 102–103

Model of communication, 3–4, **4**

Mona Lisa, **108**

Monroe, Marilyn, 46

Moral Politics (Lakoff), 34

Movement as learning, 64

Movement, authentic, 35–36

Moving an audience, 151–152, 197–208. *See also* Holding audience attention

Munk, Peter, 15

Music as pattern, 139–140

Navel and center of mass/gravity, 44–45
breathing and breath control focused on, 46–47

Needs, hierarchy of, 179–180

Negative body language habits, 19–38

Negative pressure breathing, 62–64

Negativity. *See* Pessimism

Negotiations
breath control during, 77
tension and, 153
TruthPlane positioning in, 58

Networking, 195

Neutral posture, 145

New York Times, xix

Nodding the head, 170–171

Noh theater, 205

Noise in communication, 4

Nonverbal communication, 6–7, 70

Norepinephrine reaction, 25

NoState, 159, 170–171

Objectives of message, 128–129

Office space/territory, 177, **178**

Olivier, Lawrence, 46

Optimism, 20–22

Orwell, George, 204

Oxygen, in breathing, 61–62

Oxytocin and human bonding, 27–29

Pack mentality of audience, 27–29

Paranoia, as hard-wired state, 22

Passages from Life of a Philosopher (Babbage), 3

Passionate communications, 79–93, 134
adrenaline and, 88–89
artistic representation of, 89–91
biological effects of, 82, 85–89
chest area gestures and, 83–84, 87–89
emotions associated with, 81–82
exercise in, 93
I Love You exercise in, 89
PassionPlane in, 84, **85**
trust and, 88–89
TruthPlane and, 82
universal feelings and, 82

About the Author

Mark Bowden received his university degree in performance in the U.K. and studied the gesture control methods of Jacques Lecoq's Laboratory of Movement in Paris. He worked with some of the world's most ground-breaking theater companies, appearing in multi-award-winning stage and screen productions globally and training internationally recognized actors and directors. He has worked with leading practitioners of movement psychology and built upon the influence techniques of Dr. Milton Erickson. He is the creator of TruthPlane, a unique model of training for anyone who has to communicate to an audience, and his techniques are now used by top executives and political leaders around the globe who want to gain an advantage beyond words when they speak. He has a reputation for being one of the world's expert performance trainers, and he is a highly sought-after trainer in business communication at universities including McGill and the international top 10 business school Schulich at York University in Toronto. His client list of leading businesspeople, teams, and politicians currently includes presidents and CEOs of Fortune 50 companies and prime ministers of G8 powers. He gives business presentation training to groups and keynote speeches worldwide on persuasive and influential verbal and nonverbal language and communication structures to *stand out, win trust, and profit.*

Mark can be contacted at mark@truthplane.com and followed at www.twitter.com/truthplane.

For videos and further resources to accompany this training, visit www.truthplane.com.

Chris Irwin, coauthor of the "Theory to Practice" sections, can be found via his consulting practice's site at www.MicroOB.com.

Made in the USA
Middletown, DE
06 August 2018